WINE DRINKING
for
INSPIRED THINKING

Uncork Your Creative Juices

WINE DRINKING
for
INSPIRED THINKING

Uncork Your Creative Juices

by Michael J. Gelb

RUNNING PRESS
PHILADELPHIA · LONDON

Printed in the United States

*This book may not be reproduced in whole or in part, in any form or by any means,
electronic or mechanical, including photocopying, recording, or by any information storage and re-
trieval system now known or hereafter invented, without written permission
from the publisher.*

9   8   7   6   5   4   3   2   1
Digit on the right indicates the number of this printing

Library of Congress Control Number: 20099411870

ISBN 978-0-7624-3968-6

Cover and interior design by Bill Jones
Cover photograph by Steve Legato
Illustrations by Miguel Gallardo
Edited by Jennifer Kasius
Typography: Adobe Caslon and Belucian

Running Press Book Publishers
2300 Chestnut Street
Philadelphia, PA 19103-4371

Visit us on the web!
www.runningpress.com

Picture Credits

The Merry Lute Player by Frans Hals
© Bridgeman Art Library, London / SuperStock

Bacchus by Michelangelo Buonarroti
Bargello National Museum, Florence, Italy
© SuperStock / SuperStock

Bacchus by Studio of Leonardo da Vinci
Musee du Louvre, Paris
© Peter Willi / SuperStock

Bacchus, 1596, by Michelangelo Merisi da Caravaggio
Galleria degli Uffizi, Florence, Italy
© SuperStock / SuperStock

Vitruvian Man by Leonardo da Vinci
Image © Reeed, 2009.
Used under license from Shutterstock.com.
Illustration alteration by Bill Jones.

Dedication

This book is dedicated with gratitude and love to my dad, Dr. Sanford Gelb, who introduced me to fine wine and the art of good living, and to my mom, Joan Gelb, who introduced me to the creative power of the mind.

CONTENTS

Foreword

by Karen Page and Andrew Dornenburg

We read *How to Think Like Leonardo da Vinci* when it first came out more than ten years ago. It was clear that Michael Gelb had tapped into a profound wellspring of creative power and made it accessible to readers around the world. We found the book to be inspiring and helpful in our own work as authors.

A few years later, we met Michael after Karen hosted a luncheon/book discussion for Harvard Business School alumnae and invited him to talk about his next work, *Discover Your Genius*. Michael wowed the group, and their enthusiasm prompted Karen to invite him back to speak at the organization's annual conference, where he mesmerized the crowd by sharing the principles for Thinking Like Leonardo. We soon began to explore our mutual interests of writing books and cultivating creativity and personal growth, as well as food and wine. Our friendship developed effortlessly, and like the evolution of a fine wine, it has deepened every year.

In the pages that follow you will benefit from Michael Gelb's deep knowledge of fine wine and his unique approach to sharing its enjoyment. We've experienced this approach firsthand on a number of memorable occasions. Through our dining collaborations, we have tasted some of the best wines of our lives and explored some of the most exquisite wine and food pairings. At our first dinner together in his home, Michael offered us a magnificent comparative tasting of Bordeaux with the incredible veal burgers he'd lovingly prepared for us. On another night out, we enjoyed exploring the range of Pinot Noir by comparing masterpieces from Burgundy, Oregon, and California — all paired with perfect Peking duck at Shun Lee Palace in Manhattan. We have shared many other "Holy Grail" pairings together, from Champagne and caviar to Rioja with Iberico Bellota Ham. When you read Michael's chapter on the *7 Food and Wine Pairings You Must Try Before You Die*, we can assure you that it's based on intensive, practical research in which we have been blessed to participate.

Sharing great food and wine and great ideas go hand in hand, and even more so when Michael Gelb is at the table. He brings exceptional creativity and celebratory mindfulness to the exploration of wine, food, and ideas in a way that makes him special to us and makes us excited to introduce this new book to you. We often tap Michael's knowledge for our own writing for *The Washington Post* and leading wine publications. If we need a creative quote or a pithy quip about, for example, what to drink at Thanksgiving or how various wine choices reflect personality types, Michael is at the top of our contact list. As a Renaissance Man, his breadth and depth of knowledge make him the ideal person to translate the wine experience into a unique approach to living the "Good Life."

In this book you'll get the experience of sharing this approach to the Good Life, as you learn a simple, remarkable way to inspire creativity using a right-hemisphere, poetic approach to wine. If you are new to the world of wine, you'll gain an introduction that will give you a shortcut to the essence of enjoyment. You'll learn how to handle yourself impeccably in any wine-related situation, and more than that, you'll learn how to make it fun. If you are an experienced wine aficionado, or even a professional in the world of wine, you'll gain a unique perspective that will take you, and your clients, to new dimensions of appreciation and pleasure.

In the preface, Michael cites the work of Jungian analyst Robert Johnson. Johnson suggests that our society suffers from "Dionysian Malnutrition," a deficit of natural healthy, sensual savoring of life. This book offers the nourishment we all need, through an unprecedented journey into the worlds of wine, poetry, art, and music, to correct this malady of the soul.

This poetic and artistic approach to wine and life is balanced with down-to-earth good humor and thoughtful, practical advice. For example, you'll learn how to get great value in buying wine based on Michael's easy-to-remember acronym: TIPPSY. And you'll gain an unforgettable approach to pairing food and wine by learning his WINO principles. If you work with a group of people and you want to bring them together, you'll learn a truly unique and effective approach to facilitate creativity and *esprit de corps*. And, of course, it works with friends and family too.

Like Michael Gelb's other bestselling books, *Wine Drinking for Inspired Thinking* is destined to take its place as a classic for thoughtful readers in search of wisdom and insight into the art of living. This juicy, creative book delivers its promise to help you enjoy wine and awaken your genius. You'll want to share the joy that beams from every page with the people you love.

Opening Poem:
The Spirit of Wine

by William Ernest Henley (1849—1903)

The Spirit of Wine
Sang in my glass, and I listened
With love to his odorous music,
His flushed and magnificent song.

"I am health, I am heart, I am life!
For I give for the asking
The fire of my father the Sun,
And the strength of my mother, the Earth.
Inspiration in essence,
I am wisdom and wit to the wise,
His visible muse to the poet,
The soul of desire to the lover,
The genius of laughter to all.

Come, lean on me, ye that are weary!
Rise, ye faint-hearted and doubting!
Haste, ye that lag by the way!
I am Pride, the consoler,
Valour and Hope are my henchmen,
I am the Angel of Rest.

I am life, I am wealth, I am fame:
For I captain an army
Of shining and generous dreams;
And mine, too, all mine, are the keys
Of that secret spiritual shrine,
Where, his work-a-day soul puts by,
Shut in with his saint of saints-
With his radiant and conquering self-
Man worships, and talks, and is glad.

Come, sit with me, ye that are lonely,
Ye that are paid with disdain,
Ye that are chained and would soar!
I am beauty and love;
I am friendship, the comforter;
I am that which forgives and forgets."

The Spirit of Wine
Sang in my heart, and I triumphed
In the savour and scent of his music,
His magnetic and mastering song.

Preface:
How to Drink
Like Leonardo da Vinci

"Read as you taste fruit or savor wine, or enjoy friendship, love or life."
—George Herbert (1593-1633) Welsh poet

I've never had a real job. Since 1979, I've earned my living as a self-employed creativity consultant. When people ask about my background I sometimes say that I'm a professor at M.S.U. "Ah, Michigan State University," they say. "No," I reply, "Make Stuff Up."

About fifteen years ago I made up a playful approach to appreciating wine and bringing people together. I began to share it with friends and clients, and everyone loved it. As you might imagine, specializing in creativity means that I regularly encounter skepticism, and even cynicism. (My goal is always to turn cynics into skeptics and skeptics into enthusiasts.) When people hear about the approach to wine, creativity, and camaraderie that you will learn in this book, they often have a few comments and questions, such as:

"Can I really get more creative by drinking wine?"

"You mean to tell me that you actually get paid to guide groups of people to drink wine and write poetry?"

and

"You're kidding me, right?"

The answer to these questions, respectively, is Yes, Yes, and No.

Before explaining further, I have a confession: I didn't really make this up. The credit goes to Socrates, Plato, and the other geniuses of ancient Athenian culture who created the original symposium. When you were in school and had to attend a "symposium," chances are that your teacher or professor didn't supply wine. But, the word *symposium* literally means "to drink together." Twenty-five hundred years ago, Socrates described the effect of the original symposium, when people gathered together in a convivial environment to enjoy wine and poetry: **"You will find that suddenly something extraordinary happens. As they are speaking, it's as if a spark ignites, passing from one speaker to another, and as it travels it gathers strength, building into a warm and illuminating flame of mutual understanding which none of them could have achieved alone."**

In thirty years of working with groups around the world, my greatest thrill continues to be watching the light go "on" in people's eyes when they realize that they possess the same unlimited creative power as Socrates, Leonardo, Edison, or Einstein. There's nothing quite like facilitating the spark that brings people to discover an "illuminating flame of mutual understanding…in a way none of them could have achieved alone."

In the Renaissance, great geniuses like Leonardo da Vinci facilitated a rebirth of the ancient Greek ideals of human power and potentiality. In 1998 I released a book entitled *How to Think Like Leonardo da Vinci*. The preface to that book explained, "Although it's hard to overstate Leonardo da Vinci's brilliance, recent scientific research reveals that you probably underestimate your own capabilities." In the last twelve years science has demonstrated even more convincingly that you were born with a virtually unlimited capacity for creativity. Moreover, your brain is designed to improve with use, and your one hundred billion neurons are capable of making more connections than the number of atoms that exist in the entire universe. Neuroscientists refer to the ability of the brain to continually reinvent itself as *neuroplasticity*. In other words, we now know that you can continue to develop your intelligence throughout your life, and we also know that there are different types of intelligence. In this book we will focus on a playful, wine-inspired approach to developing three aspects of intelligence. They are:

Sensory Intelligence: The ability to observe and process sensory information with speed and accuracy. Sensory acuity can be consciously cultivated throughout life, and wine appreciation is an ideal way to do it. Leonardo da Vinci's term for sensory intelligence is Sensazione. He noted that the five senses are "the ministers of the soul."

Creative Intelligence: The ability to generate ideas rapidly and fluidly, to think analogically and metaphorically, and to be able to view problems from multiple perspectives. Reading and writing poetry is one of the simplest and most effective means for nurturing creative intelligence. (And experience demonstrates that people write better poetry after a couple of glasses of good wine.)

Social Intelligence: The ability to act wisely in social situations, to get along with others by practicing accurate empathy. Also known as interpersonal intelligence, this is one of the most important elements in a successful and fulfilling life. Sharing wine and poetry is a pleasurable way to cultivate the empathy, intuition and sensitivity that make you more socially intelligent.

Leonardo was a genius in all these areas. Five centuries ago, he invented the parachute, before anyone could fly. That's thinking ahead! Leonardo wrote, "The love of anything is the fruit of our knowledge of it, and grows as our knowledge deepens." These words are certainly true about wine, which Leonardo referred to as "the divine juice of the grape." As my knowledge of wine has deepened over the years, my love for the divine juice has grown, and so has my passion for sharing it with others. One of the fruits of my passion is this approach to appreciating wine as a means to encourage the development of the potential everyone has to be more creative and intuitive, to think more like Leonardo.

My mission to inspire creative thinking has led me to ask thousands of people this question: *Where are you physically located when you get your best ideas?*

Most people respond that they get their best ideas in the shower, while driving, or resting in bed.

The idea for this book arose at around 4 a.m., when I was musing in bed after a wonderful evening of wine and poetry shared with a group of twenty-four people. This particular group wasn't especially knowledgeable about wine, and they certainly didn't think of themselves as poetic, so they were a bit taken aback when they learned that we would be expressing our experience of wine in poetic terms, and that prizes would be awarded for the most evocative poems. But, just as Socrates described it, something magical took place. Besides enjoying a fabulous evening of laughter and camaraderie, everyone in the group gained a sense of the transformational power of the divine juice—and they rose to the occasion, surprising themselves by generating remarkably inspiring verse.

In that early morning hour, I became intoxicated with the notion of sharing this creative juice with you. I reflected on the smiling faces of various friends, clients, and associates as they experienced this approach to wine drinking for inspired thinking. And I recalled the enthusiastic responses from all kinds of people, such as the professor from a leading business school who exclaimed:

"That's the most fun we've ever had together as a faculty in the thirty years I've been here!"

And the sponsor of this event for a group of entrepreneurs and their spouses, who wrote:

"The combination of wine and poetry inspired our group, and literally drew joyful tears from many of our members. It was an evening we will never forget."

This soul-enlivening approach to enjoying wine had to be shared with a wider circle than just the friends who come to my home for wine and poetry salons or those groups who engage my services directly. The next day, when I mentioned the idea to one of my wine- drinking friends, she responded: "At last, how to *drink* like Leonardo da Vinci."

Although there are many excellent guides to wine appreciation, the "whole-brain" creative approach you'll enjoy in these pages is different. In addition to learning the left-brain strategies for finding great wine values and managing all kinds of wine-related situations, you'll also experience a right-brain way to bring more joy and fun to the exploration of wine. As you learn to use the appropriate dose of wine to liberate your muse, you will discover that you are much more creative than you may have imagined.

You will also learn a simple, playful approach for bringing people together with wine and poetry. You can do it with your friends and family to inspire conviviality and pure joy. If you work in a corporation, non-profit organization, or as part of any kind of team, you'll learn how to bring people together in a way that encourages creative collaboration and camaraderie. And you don't have to attend a certification program to learn how to do it. Just read and drink!

Overcoming Dionysian Malnutrition

Scorch-the-Earth, exploit-the-worker types usually don't hire me. My clients tend to be visionary, humanistic leaders who are devoted to developing the creative potential of their people. But even in the most creative and humanistic organizations, there's been an increasing level of pressure, stress, and angst.

When I started leading seminars in the late 1970s, groups usually devoted five full days to the process. Now it's hard to get people away from the office for a day. Every aspect of organizational life is subject to metrics and evaluation, and the pressure to get more results in less time with fewer resources continues to mount. As a client from a pharmaceutical company recently commented:

I'm working harder than ever before. When we finish one project there's no time to celebrate because the pressure is on to complete the next one.

A manager from a software firm shared this poignant sentiment:

I get up, take a swig of morning coffee, get the kids off to school, fight morning traffic, get to the office. My entire life seems pre-programmed.

And a human resources director observed,

Things were getting grim and tight before the economic downturn, and now it seems that there's no place at all for fun and joy. How did we get to be so out of touch?

In *Ecstasy: Understanding the Psychology of Joy,* Jungian analyst Robert A. Johnson explains, "Our society esteems thinking and doing, progress and success, above all else. We go straight ahead, aiming for the top, looking out for number one in all our endeavors. If a given thing does not have a monetary value, or show a concrete return, we will probably place it lower on the scale. We tend to like those things we can control and dislike what we can't control."

Of course, order, progress, results, and success are important, but as the need to measure, standardize, analyze, and control becomes ever more dominant, the soul tends to suffer. If we neglect joy, we lose touch with the intangible realms of intuition, empathy, receptivity, and creativity.

Our organizations and our society at large suffer from what Johnson calls "Dionysian Malnutrition." Dionysus is the Greek god of wine and joy. He represents the primal life force.

In contemporary literature, the primal force of Dionysus is best expressed in the novel *Zorba the Greek* by Nikos Kazantzakis (1883–1957). Zorba (played by Anthony Quinn in the movie) enthuses to Basil (played by Alan Bates) about the transformational power of wine. He declares that wine is a miraculous creative juice that expands the soul, a means for transcending the small-mindedness and egotism of the daily grind. Basil pours more wine, clinks glasses with Zorba and reflects,

"The world was recovering its pristine freshness. All the dulled daily things regained the brightness that they had in the beginning."

When the pristine freshness of our connection with this Dionysian spirit is repressed, when the soul's yearning for contact, celebration, and beauty is denied, then it resurfaces as one form or another of addictive behavior. A recent internet search on the term *Rehab* yielded more than 45 million results. Our culture worships celebrities, our substitutes for the gods of Olympus, and the stories of their addictions, recoveries, and relapses. This imbalance also manifests in the pandemic of obesity. A recent study, trumpeted on all the major networks, proclaimed, "If current trends hold, researchers from Johns Hopkins University say, nearly *all* American adults will be overweight or obese by the year 2030." And, in the realm of sexuality, things are even crazier.

We are subject to an endless onslaught of polarizing images, lurching between obesity and anorexia, pornography and repression, drunkenness and abstemiousness.

Images and models of healthy pleasure are rare.

On an individual basis we all seek balance between the pressures and demands of our sometimes neurotic world and our desire for wellness, pleasure, and relaxation.

Socrates, Leonardo, Einstein, and Edison all understood that relaxation opened the gate to the vast potential of the mind that is beyond the ordinary IQ. Socrates did it with wine and poetry. Edison took naps on his desk and retreated to a nearby fishing hole, where he fished with a baitless hook. Einstein walked in nature and played imagination games. Leonardo told the Duke of Milan that he needed to take time away from his intense labor on *The Last Supper* to allow his intuitive intelligence to process the work in a receptive state. The Maestro explained: "Men of genius sometimes work best when they work least."

Men and women of genius understand that relaxation, receptivity, and creativity go together. Rather than repressing the Dionysian spirit, we can befriend it and discover a life affirming, healthy relationship to sex, food, wine, and ourselves.

Maybe this all sounds like too much fun? But, as you've probably noticed, despite the increasing pressures of work life, old paradigms are beginning to shift. Many people are recognizing that the need for innovation requires us to soften the rigid boundaries between work and play. The wise have always understood that the best thinking emerges from a passionate sense of play. The ancient Greek philosopher Heraclitus emphasized, "We are most nearly ourselves when we achieve the seriousness of the child at play." Learning creative ways to relax and play with your friends or colleagues offers serious benefits. John Cleese, star of *Fawlty Towers* and the Food Network show *Wine for the Confused* explains, "The essence of creativity is not the possession of some special talent, it is much more the ability to play."

In the pages that follow, you will learn to bring more joy to your life and awaken your creativity through a playful approach to appreciating wine. As you learn to dance with Dionysus, you will also discover a way to deepen your appreciation for the soulful brilliance of your family, friends, and colleagues.

Uniting Pleasure and Truth

The motto for our journey is provided by the literary genius Dr. Samuel Johnson (1709-1784) who defined poetry as, "The art of uniting pleasure with truth." The truth is that the appropriate dose of pleasure will improve your ability to think creatively and effectively. The overemphasis on the "nose to the grindstone, shoulder to the wheel" attitude that still drives so many lives often results in flatter noses and frozen shoulders.

The approach to wine and creativity in this book is based on a few fundamental assumptions we will explore together. These include the following notions:

• Your potential for creative intelligence is virtually unlimited, and you can learn to tap that potential to enrich your life.
• The enjoyment of wine, in moderation, can be an integral element in a healthy, happy, and creative life.
• The appropriate amount of wine in the right setting serves to

gently inhibit left-brain functioning and to liberate the more imaginative right brain. We can take advantage of this to explore and enjoy the more poetic aspects of our being.

• Pleasure, joy, relaxation, and the appreciation of beauty go hand in hand and all serve to enrich sensory intelligence, nourish the soul, and inspire creativity.

• Creativity, joy, wine, and poetry are all more fun when they are shared. As we share these elements, we can enhance our interpersonal intelligence, deepen our social bonds, and strengthen esprit de corps.

This approach challenges the common assumption that gain is only obtained through pain. Hard work, diligence, and perseverance are essential elements in long-term success. but they need to be balanced with appreciation of beauty, playfulness, pleasure, and joy to ensure that success includes fulfillment.

We also reject the common notion of wine as something that harms the body and dulls the mind. Wine and other forms of alcohol are, of course, subject to misuse, often with devastating effect. Our approach is based on the idea that moderate, mindful consumption of wine offers many benefits to body, mind, and spirit.

When you open a bottle of wine and share it with your friends or colleagues, you are expressing your connection with an ancient, vivifying cultural practice. You are linking, as we shall see, with a tradition that has inspired many of the greatest minds in human history, including Socrates and Plato, Leonardo and Michelangelo, and Franklin and Jefferson.

Of course, sharing wine and poetry won't directly solve your most important problems, but when approached in the simple framework you will learn they will help you celebrate life; deepen bonds with family, friends, and colleagues; uncork your creative juices; and think in new ways.

How to Enjoy This Book

Wine rejoices the heart of man, and joy
is the mother of all virtue.
—Johann Wolfgang von Goethe (1749-1832)

I was recently blessed with the opportunity to stay at the Four Seasons Hotel in Vancouver, British Columbia. The hotel offered a fabulous brunch buffet, included in the price of the room. Before filling my plate, I walked around and surveyed all of the delicacies. Although the buffet was organized in progressive stations focusing on appetizers, entrees, and desserts, I decided to create my own order for optimal enjoyment, and that's just how I suggest you approach this book. Scan through the whole book first and then decide where you want to start and the order in which you'd like to taste each chapter.

If you want to begin by drinking immediately, please get a good bottle or two and go directly to the chapter "Sensazione-7: The Art of Tasting," where you can explore multi-sensory, right-hemisphere wine appreciation. If you are keen to learn about the practical business of wine etiquette, go straight to "Mastering Wine-lists, Sommeliers, Snobs, Corks, and Etiquette." If you can't wait to discover a great strategy for buying wine and finding super values, feel free to begin with another chapter in Part 1: "TIPPSY: A Wine Buying Strategy." If your primary passion is matching food and wine, there's no reason not to go immediately to these chapters: "The WINO Principles: Matching Food and Wine" and "The 7 Wine and Food Pairings You Must Experience Before You Die."

If you are most intrigued by the notion of the confluence of wine and genius and the relationship between wine and art, architecture, and music, begin by savoring Part 2: "The Elixir of Genius." If you want to conduct a New Symposium wine and poetry event with a group and you can't wait to learn how to do it, jump ahead to Part 3: "The New Symposium." If you'd prefer to begin by enjoying some of the world's great wine-related poetry then please don't hesitate to go to the chapter on the "All-Time Wine Poetry Prize Winners."

You can also enjoy this book in good old linear fashion. The introductory chapters explain the evolution of this unusual approach to cultivating creative thinking by drinking. The introduction also aims to establish a context for the enjoyment of wine as an integral part of a healthy and creative life. As you read, you may come across unfamiliar wine terms— if you want the definition and some background you can look them up in the Wine Geek Jargon Guide in Part 4. Part 4 also includes an extensive, annotated list of resources for further learning and enjoyment. (Including a website that provides hotlinks to all the sites mentioned in the book).

This book is for you whether you are new to the world of wine or a seasoned aficionado. Regardless of your level of experience, and whatever path you choose to take through these pages, my wish is to inspire you to a deeper appreciation of wine, life, and the beauty of your creative essence.

Cheers!

—Michael J. Gelb, November 2009

Introduction:
From Happy Hour
to La Dolce Vita

*Wine- one sip of this will bathe the drooping
spirits in delight beyond the bliss of dreams.
Be wise and taste.*
—John Milton (1608-1674)

La dolce vita is Italian for "the sweet, soulful life." The French have something similar called *joie de vivre*, which means "the joy of living." But what do we have in the States?

Happy Hour?

Miller Time?

We need help.

In Italy, most folks have a greater sense of history than those of us in the United States. After all, they're descendants of the Romans, and although modern Italy is young as a unified country, the sense of connection with history is profound. Italian culture also places more emphasis on savoring the present moment, especially when dining. At lunchtime, for example, everything stops when the steaming bowl of pasta is presented with some fresh tomato sauce, a hint of garlic and basil, and perhaps a dusting of grated pecorino cheese and a few flakes of hot red pepper.

And, there always seems to be time to appreciate the color and aroma of the Chianti, time to breathe, time to be. Of course, it helps to be surrounded by the magical Tuscan light illuminating the vineyards, and fields of lavender flecked with dancing white butterflies, but this same sense of presence and enjoyment is evident in a busy trattoria in the center of Rome or Florence.

In the States many people don't bother with lunch. They "grab a bite" on the run. And they aren't as aware of history. But they are focused on the future. The important point is that we live in a world that is increasingly linked, and we have an unprecedented opportunity to incorporate the lessons of history from diverse cultures and traditions while preparing for a better future for ourselves, our families, our organizations, and our communities. The missing link for many is the ability to savor the present moment.

The appreciation of fine wine is a passport to the present moment. A simple way to put more *dolce* in your *vita*. A daily blessing. As Einstein commented: "There are 2 ways to live your life: one is as though nothing is a miracle, the other is as though everything is a miracle."

Miraculously, there are more great wines today from more parts of the world than ever before. You can travel the globe without leaving your table. Your glass can be filled with the essence of the soil, sun, and soul of diverse regions of the earth, from Australia's Barossa Valley to Spain's Ribera del Duero, from Santa Barbara to St. Emillion. Fine wine is art you can drink, liquid poetry that, when read in the right spirit, will transport you to new realms of presence, conviviality, and joy.

Putting More Dolce in Your Vita

Leonardo da Vinci wrote, "The lover is to the beloved as the sense is to that which it perceives." He trained his sensory awareness like an Olympic athlete trains his body for competition. But five-hundred years ago, in Tuscany, Leonardo reflected that the average person "looks without seeing, listens without hearing, touches without feeling, eats without tasting, moves without physical awareness, inhales without awareness of odor or fragrance, and talks without thinking."

Today, the challenge to achieve refined sensory awareness is much greater. Without a conscious discipline for cultivating sensory awareness, we are all subject to the numbing effects of the lowest-common-denominator, mass-market McWorld. How can we navigate through the tsunami of spam, sharpen our senses, and enrich the quality of our lives? Start by surrounding yourself with beauty: savor sunsets, keep fresh flowers in your office, listen to Mozart, go to the art museum, and always drink the very best wine that you can afford.

In the following pages you will learn a simple approach to deepening your everyday sense of beauty, joy, and celebration. You will discover a delightful way to enjoy wine and liberate your creativity. In order to do this with your family and friends or for your colleagues at work it helps to know how to choose, purchase, and appreciate fine wine.

In Part 1, you will learn simple, practical, and memorable strategies for navigating through the world of wine, with a special emphasis on finding great values. Wine etiquette is becoming an increasingly important part of social and professional life, so you will be guided to a sense of ease and mastery in those situations. **After reading this book you will be forever free from intimidation in any wine-related situation.** You will gain a sense of confidence in your ability to delight your family, friends, clients and colleagues with your oenological insight. You will also enjoy a simple, delicious approach to the art of matching food and wine, including a discussion of seven great food-wine pairings that you must experience before you die.

This book is more than just a guide to navigating through the world of wine. It offers a uniquely powerful avenue to liberating your creative juices. In addition to a thorough grounding in the left-brain knowledge necessary **to find great value wines**, Part 1 also introduces you to a creative, right-brain way to enjoy wine that will help you to **get**

much more value out of every wine experience. This approach instantly takes the fear out of wine exploration and multiplies the fun.

In Part 2, we will take a wine-soaked journey through the history of genius, including an introduction to some of the greatest wine-related art, music, and architecture. You'll discover how wine has served as a catalyst for creativity through the ages, and you'll deepen your sense of connection to this enlightened wave of culture. In Part 3 you'll be guided, step-by-step, through **a delightful process for bringing your family, friends, or colleagues together,** applying a contemporary version of the ancient Greek symposium. Robert Louis Stevenson (1850-1894) referred to wine as "bottled poetry." **You will learn to release the poetry from the bottle and uncork the creative juices that have been bottled-up within you.**

The final part of the book offers a guide to some of the world's best wine resources: books, educators, and critics, and how to benefit from their wisdom. It also includes a "Wine Geek Jargon Guide," where you will find colorful definitions and explanations of the wine terms used in the book.

Let's set the stage for this delightful exploration of *la dolce vita* with some further background on the evolution of this approach.

From Passaic to the Poet Laureate

"The flavor of wine is like delicate poetry."
—Louis Pasteur (1822-1895)

Sandy, my dad, adores my mom, Joan. They've been married for almost sixty years. Sandy is a very romantic guy, and he's always looking for creative ways to express his love. In the early 1960s his practice as an oral surgeon began to thrive, and he decided to celebrate by taking Joan to the 35 Club near Passaic, New Jersey. As he expresses it, "I wanted to be a big sport and treat your mother to something really special." He adds, "I didn't know anything about wine, but I had heard of Mouton Rothschild, so I ordered the most expensive half-bottle of wine on the list: A 1959 Chateau Mouton Rothschild for nine dollars."

They liked it. Shortly thereafter Sandy read a series of articles by the legendary wine educator Alexis Bespaloff, and he enrolled in a wine appreciation class at the Four Seasons restaurant in New York. He invested in good wine glasses, a decanter, and he started to bring home fine wines for us to try with dinner. He also brought his tasting notes and a long list of adjectives for articulating the experience of wine tasting. My younger brothers and I were introduced to classic wine description terms such as, "earthy," "plummy," "tight," "tannic," "supple," and "silky." We had great fun teasing my dad and making up our own wacky descriptors. As with most things, however, we all paid careful attention to Mom's critiques. She has an uncanny ability to accurately criticize everything, from theater and literature to fashion and character. Mom was the supreme arbiter of taste, and Dad was always seeking to inspire her to rapture.

One evening, Sandy brought home a wine that we could tell, from the manner in which he cradled the bottle, must be very special. He explained that it was a mature Bordeaux and proceeded to decant it with great care. Most of the wines we had tried were relatively young, so this was to be a new experience. He poured little tastes for us and full glasses for himself and Joan. We watched as he swirled the wine in his glass and savored the aroma. He sipped, rolled the wine around his palate, and then swallowed. He seemed pleased, but all eyes shifted to Mom. She took a quick whiff and a small sip and rendered her assessment in one word: "Menopausal." We all cracked up. As usual, she was right, as the wine had, indeed, passed its prime.

Joan now states that she no longer finds her quip to be so amusing, but she agrees that our early experiences of describing and discussing wines served to deepen our appreciation and bring our family together. Although as a teenager I was far more engaged in thinking about girls than vintages, I nevertheless developed a sense that wine offered a

magic all its own.

Despite my early introduction to fine wines, I confess that in college I drank my share of Boone's Farm, Mateus, and even Shopper's Paradise Tawny Port ($4 per gallon!). Then, when I turned thirty, I realized, as my dad had years before, that I was now earning a decent living and could afford to buy my own wine. Fortunately, my thirtieth year was 1982, a legendary, benchmark vintage for Bordeaux. My wine collection was initiated with "futures" ordered from some of the greatest estates. I participated in wine seminars and classes and began reading and tasting voraciously.

In addition to enriching the depth of pleasure in my personal life, the appreciation of wine proved to be very useful professionally. I led many seminars in Europe and often bonded with clients through sharing and enjoying fine wine. Wine was clearly a delightful catalyst for inspiring creativity and bringing people together, as well as an intrinsic part of the good life. As Ernest Hemingway (1899-1961) observed, "In Europe we thought of wine as something as healthy and normal as food and also a great giver of happiness and well-being and delight. Drinking wine was not a snobbism nor a sign of sophistication nor a cult; it was as natural as eating and to me as necessary."

But, except in parts of California and a few other places in the United States, "wine culture" was lacking, and many of my friends and clients in the States were unfamiliar and uncomfortable in the world of wine. I began "adding value" for clients by leading wine-tastings during dinner after a day of training in creative thinking. Many friends and clients began asking for help in selecting wines, and it wasn't unusual for me to get a call asking for guidance in what to choose from a wine list. I sought to help my friends and clients find wines that were high quality and superb value, and the emphasis on quality and value was, of course, especially relevant in business situations.

Then, in the mid-'90s, I was asked to be co-director of a series of three-week leadership development programs for a global investment bank. This intensive team-building program was the brainchild of creative thinking pioneer Tony Buzan. Buzan, an accomplished poet and wine aficionado, invited British Poet-Laureate Ted Hughes to be part of the faculty. I was blessed with the opportunity to attend Ted's poetry classes and to share many fine wines with Tony and Ted.

Why was the British Poet -Laureate invited to teach at a seminar for bankers? Well, they loved his classes, and the experience of culti-vating poetic awareness strengthened the group's ability to think more creatively. Listening to Ted read his poems, we all became aware of the ability of a well-chosen word to inspire a multitude of feelings, images, sounds, tastes, and smells. Ted wrote a poem, for example, about a jaguar (not the car). When he said the word *JAG-U-ARRRRR* he evoked more than just the predator's terrifying growl, but also the sense of its sinuous body stalking through the jungle. The more our senses were stimulated, the more memorable each word became. I was famil-iar with the role of the merging and cross-referencing of the senses in the creative process, but working with Ted helped me take this appre-ciation to a deeper plane.

Multi-Sensory Awareness

What do Nobel Prize-winning physicist Richard Feynman (1918-1988), abstract painting pioneer Wassily Kandinsky (1866-1944), legendary jazz innovator Miles Davis (1926-1991), and Robert Parker Jr. (1947-), the world's most influ-ential wine critic, all have in common?

The merging or cross-referencing of the senses. Also known as synesthesia, this ability is a notable characteristic of great scientists, artists, musicians, poets, and connoisseurs.

You can cultivate your own creativity by developing multi-sen-sory awareness. In the process, you will enrich your apprecia-tion and enjoyment of art, music, and wine. As you learn to express your experience of aromas and tastes, for example, in palettes of color and musical associations, your appreciation, enjoyment, and recall for the tastes and aromas deepens dramatically. Robert Parker Jr. describes his multi-sensory approach: "A wine goes in my mouth, and I just see it. I see it in three dimensions. The textures. The flavors. The smells. They just jump out at me."

I was also honored that Ted attended my lectures on thinking like Leonardo. Having him in my class was both humbling and inspiring. At the time, I was still working on the manuscript of *How to Think Like Leonardo da Vinci*, and I was exploring ways to communicate the principles for thinking like the Maestro. As part of my research, I traveled to Italy and was blessed with many wonderful experiences of la dolce vita, including an opportunity to dine at the Antinori family winery. The Antinori were established winemakers when Leonardo was growing up in Florence. We tasted their extraordinary wines and dined on ravioli made with flour from the family's wheat fields, cheese from their cows, and olive oil from their groves.

Beyond exploring the great wines and vineyards of Tuscany, I spent weeks in Napa and Sonoma, the Loire Valley, Bordeaux, and my favorite: the Langhe region of northern Italy. I've been blessed by the opportunity to taste wines with some of the great winemakers of the world and to learn from many of the world's great wine educators.

So, after spending time with Ted Hughes, meeting many of the finest wine makers and educators and visiting the world's great vineyards, and introducing people around the world to the principles for thinking like Leonardo, I naturally began to express my passion for wine in poetic terms. But the real fun began when I got my friends and clients to start writing poetry about wine.

Why poetry? I was inspired to inspire others toward a more poetic, right-brained approach to wine because, as I attended a variety of wine-related events—tastings, dinners, seminars—it was apparent that many folks took the proceedings, and themselves, much too seriously. Just like many seminars on classical music or art appreciation, participants often seemed to indulge in one-upmanship and snobbery. Pretension was rife, and many people seemed to be driven by the fear of making mistakes. Although the best educators, like Kevin Zraly, always included a hearty dose of humor, this was more the exception than the rule. The majority of wine education events were just plain boring, suffering from an overly analytical "left-brain" approach. Moreover, I sensed that a more experimental approach to appreciating wine might be helpful in encouraging people to think outside the box.

Better Business by Brunello

High-powered CEO Cheryl Rosner has a remarkable record helping companies such as Expedia Corporate Travel and Hotels.com achieve unprecedented success. Named one of the "25 Most Influential People in Travel" by *Business Travel News* in 2004, Rosner is a powerhouse of creative, strategic thinking. How does she find her muse? "Brunello," she explains. "I get my best ideas when I relax with a bottle of fine wine." Rosner's most recent breakthrough idea for her business came after enjoying the 1999 Poggio Antico Brunello di Montalcino. She was so inspired by the wine that she sent a bottle to each member of her team. As she says, "There's something transformational about great wine in the right setting."

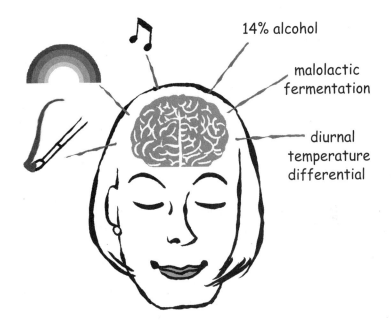

14% alcohol

malolactic
fermentation

diurnal
temperature
differential

Out of the Box: Drinking and Thinking

See! I clasp the cup whose power
Yields more wisdom in an hour
Than whole years of study give,
Vainly seeking how to live.
Wine dispenses into air
Selfish thoughts, and selfish care.
Dost thou know why wine I prize?
He who drinks all ill defies

—Omar Khayyam, Persian poet (1048-1142)
on wine drinking for inspired thinking

The best wine isn't usually found in a box. And the same thing is true with thinking.

When it comes to thinking, "the box" that everyone wants to escape has its place. "Box thinking" is a function of the left-hemisphere of the cerebral cortex. It is logical, organized, and essential for an orderly life. The problem is that most of us are so habituated to this way of thinking that we don't know how to do any other kind.

Professor Roger Sperry (1913 -1994), Nobel Laureate in Medicine and Physiology, referred to this limiting tendency when he wrote, "Our educational system, and modern society generally, discriminates against one whole half of the brain. In our present educational system, the attention given to the right hemisphere is minimal, compared to the training lavished on the left side." Sperry emphasizes that most of our schooling is biased to the left. (And this includes most attempts to learn about wine.) Moreover, many people find that their ability to innovate is limited by this habitual bias. How do we learn to think out of the box and then integrate that creative thinking into reality?

Creative, "out-of-the-box" thinking involves generating and exploring lots of new ideas, thinking analogically and metaphorically, and nurturing different perspectives. This kind of thinking is much easier to do when we relax, let go of our preconceptions, and begin to engage the imagination. For the last thirty years I've been exploring the most effective means for helping people relax, let go, and engage the other half of the brain. Sharing wine and poetry is at the top of the list. It is a delightful and creative way to liberate the muse and free us from the habit of using only half the mind.

When it comes to using the whole mind in balance, Leonardo da Vinci offers a perfect role model. Renowned for his art and science, Leonardo integrated the left and right brain. A great scientist, Leonardo was a pioneer in anatomy, botany, and physics. He insisted that his students understand mathematics and science, and he cautioned that without a proper grounding in anatomy, for example, "the muscles and bones that you draw will look like bunches of nuts and radishes."

Leonardo is also renowned for the unparalleled creativity in his drawings, paintings, and inventions. In his notebooks he offers advice on "quickening the spirit of invention." He suggests contemplating abstract forms like clouds in the sky, or smoke rising from a fire, and counsels letting the mind go free. The Maestro explains, "You will see in these an infinity of things—divine landscapes, which you may then reduce to their complete and proper forms." In the thousand years prior to Leonardo, the idea of "letting the mind go free" wasn't very popular with church authorities in Europe. But Leonardo effectively invented what we now call creative thinking.

Leonardo understood that in order to create we must first generate (let the mind go free) and then organize (reduce to complete and proper forms). "Left-brain bias" results in a tendency to organize ideas prematurely. Leonardo counsels you to overcome premature organization, get out of the box, and liberate your muse by cultivating the ability to generate first, then organize.

This ability is expressed in the writer's motto "Write drunk, revise sober."

"Write drunk" refers to the right-hemisphere generated process of letting go and free associating, exploring lots of ideas. "Revise sober" refers to the left-hemisphere challenge of editing, organizing, and implementing those ideas. If you write and revise sober, your work is boring, and no one wants to read it. If you write and revise drunk, no one can read it.

Wine is favorable to the play of invention

G. C. Lichtenberg (1742-1799) was the first person to hold a chair in experimental physics at a German university. Admired as an independent thinker by Kant and Goethe and later by Nietzsche and Freud, Lichtenberg was inducted into the Royal Society in 1793. Renowned for the aphorisms recorded in his notebooks, Lichtenberg takes the notion of "Write drunk, revise sober" literally. He noted: "There is no harm in doing one's thinking while slightly drunk, and then revising one's work in cold blood. The stimulus of wine is favorable to the play of invention and to fluency of expression."

In her book *My Stroke of Insight: A Brain Scientist's Personal Journey,* Dr. Jill Bolte Taylor offers a dramatic, inspiring example of the power of getting out of the box. On December 10, 1996, a blood vessel in the left hemisphere of Taylor's brain exploded. For most people this would be a disaster, but for Taylor, a Harvard-trained neuroscientist, it was the opportunity of a lifetime. She writes, "How many brain scientists have been able to study the brain from the inside out? I've gotten as much out of this experience of losing my left mind as I have in my entire academic career." Taylor observed while her left hemisphere, responsible for linear processing, language, organizing, and planning, began to shut down. She experienced what she describes as a state of "nirvana" in which she was "captivated by the magnificence around me." Taylor's right-hemisphere epiphany included a greater awareness of sights, sounds, feelings, and aromas; a profound sense of participation in the present moment without worry about the past or future; and a sense of euphoric connectedness and love for all creation.

Taylor's book describes her journey to regain her lost functions while nurturing her new creative awareness. More than just a guide for recovering stroke patients, Taylor offers an inspiring example for everyone interested in living a fuller, more creative life. She invites her readers to "choose to step to the right of their left hemispheres."

The right dose of fine wine and poetry offers a simple, everyday way to accept Taylor's invitation to relax our hyperactive left minds and open to the out-of-the box right mind.

Daniel Pink, author of *A Whole New Mind: Why Right-Brainers Will Rule the Future,* explains, "The future belongs to a very different kind of person with a very different kind of mind. The era of left-brain dominance, and the Information Age that it engendered, is giving way to a new world in which right-brain qualities—inventiveness, empathy, meaning—predominate." Pink emphasizes that creative thinking, emotional intelligence and collaboration are more important than ever; he adds, "the wine and poetry exercise described in these pages is a beautiful way to unify these abilities."

In Part 1, you will develop the left hemisphere savvy you need to master the essentials of practical wine knowledge and etiquette. You will also be introduced to an out-of-the-box approach to right-hemisphere wine appreciation that will deepen your enjoyment dramatically.

But first, let's summarize the research on the role of wine in a healthy life.

Whole-Brain Winemaking

"The wine maker must be a scientist and a poet."
Craig Williams, Vintner of the 2002 Joseph Phelps Insignia, *Wine Spectator* Wine of the Year, in 2005.

Wine and Health:
The Power of Positive Drinking

"In vino sanitas"
("In wine there is health")
—Pliny the Elder (23-79 A.D.)
Roman philosopher and naturalist

Growing up in Passaic, New Jersey, my earliest association with wine was with "winos," a.k.a. "bums" and "drunks," the unfortunate denizens of "Skid Row" and "The Bowery." Before my dad started to teach us about fine wine, I assumed that all forms of alcohol were unhealthy. As Sandy followed his passion, he founded a club, along with my uncle and some of their friends, to explore great combinations of food and wine. All of the founding members of the club were medical professionals. It became apparent, as I learned more about wine, that in the proper proportion it was a veritable health tonic. Over the years, I've observed that many of the most passionate collectors and connoisseurs are, like my dad and his club members, doctors.

I've always been passionate about health and fitness. Part of my fascination with Leonardo da Vinci is that, in addition to his talents as an artist and scientist, he was renowned for his physical gifts and his insights into health and wellness. Leonardo embodied the principles of balance and proportionality expressed in his art. His exquisite *Vitruvian Man* continues to serve as a universal image of health and wholeness five hundred years after he drew it as an illustration for his friend's book on "Divine Proportion."

Leonardo's advice on health and wellness is as relevant today as it was when he first shared it in his notebook. He wrote, "Learn to preserve your own health." This, of course, is the essence of modern holistic health, a philosophy based on the notion that we take

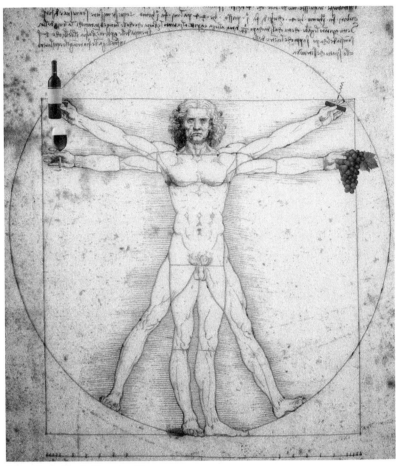

Leonardo da Vinci's *Vitruvian Man*

responsibility for our own well-being. Leonardo championed the classical notion *mens sana in corpore sano* —a healthy mind in a healthy body. As part of this approach, he counseled the enjoyment of wine, in moderation, with meals.

Of course, the notion that wine is good for the health of body and mind pre-dates the Renaissance. More than two thousand years before Leonardo, Homer praised its power in restoring strength, and Hippocrates made wine a part of most of his prescriptions. The Jewish Talmud notes, "Wherever wine is lacking, drugs become necessary," and the Talmud also proclaims, "At the head of all medical remedies am I, wine." In the New Testament, Paul's letter to Timothy advises, " No longer drink only water, but use a little wine for the sake of your stomach and your other ailments."

Wine historian Hugh Johnson quotes a sixth century Indian medical text that refers to wine as the "invigorator of mind and body, antidote to sleeplessness, sorrow, and fatigue...producer of hunger, happiness, and digestion." The Dutch humanist scholar Desiderius Erasmus (1466 -1536) proclaimed, "Wine [is] the most profitable medicine and pleasant repast, nothing hurtful moderately taken." The great Louis Pasteur (1822-1895) called wine "the most healthful and most hygienic of beverages." Sir Alexander Fleming (1881-1955), the discoverer of penicillin, commented, "If penicillin can cure those that are ill, Spanish sherry can bring the dead back to life."

Benjamin Franklin, George Washington, John Adams, and Thomas Jefferson all believed in the health benefits of moderate wine consumption. As Jefferson observed: "Wine from long habit has become indispensable for my health."

Given this historical wisdom about the benefits of wine, it's amazing to remember that from 1920 to 1933 it was illegal to order a bottle of wine with dinner in the United States of America. Prohibition was a disaster. It facilitated the rise of organized crime and created general disrespect for the rule of law. The rate of alcoholism in the country actually rose during this period. Although the Volstead Act was repealed in 1933, those thirteen years colored the perspective of citizens in general and doctors in particular in regard to the effects of wine on health. Even now, every bottle of wine sold in the United States features a government-mandated warning label that states that the contents "may cause health problems."

Common sense dictates that it's wise for pregnant women to avoid alcohol and for everyone to avoid drinking and driving, but abstaining from wine altogether "may cause health problems." As Dr. R. Curtis Ellison, Professor of Medicine & Public Health at Boston University School of Medicine, comments, "Abstinence is a risk factor."

Ellison, who is also a senior researcher with the sixty year effort to understand the risk factors for heart disease known as the Framingham Heart Study, explains that as an epidemiologist and a wine lover, he has devoted considerable time and energy to reviewing the literature on the health effects of wine. He recently told *Wine Spectator*, "Moderate wine consumption can safely add pleasure to life. More significantly, it can also reduce our risks of falling prey to many of the most common health hazards of contemporary life, including heart disease, stroke, dementia, and even obesity. On balance, I believe moderate wine consumption can be a vital element of a lifestyle that will help us lead longer, healthier lives."

In the United States, the turning point in terms of broad understanding of the potential benefits of wine for health was the November 1991, *60 Minutes* television report on the "French Paradox." *60 Minutes* reported that although people in southern France ate significant amounts of fatty, high-cholesterol foods such as butter, cream, cheese, and meat, they appeared to have lower incidences of heart disease than Americans. Researchers posited that it was the regular consumption of red wine (and olive oil) that made the difference.

The American Paradox

The American Paradox is a term coined by Michael Pollan, author of *The Omnivore's Dilemma*. He suggests that given the amount of junk food eaten "on the run" without mindfulness, and, without olive oil or red wine, it's amazing that Americans live as long as we do.

Since 1991 there's been an explosion of interest in the potential health benefits of wine. Researchers have conducted thousands of studies around the world with many different populations. The most reliable and significant findings all focus on the potential benefits of regular, moderate consumption of red wine to help:

- prevent Alzheimer's and other forms of dementia
- avoid cardio-vascular and coronary disease
- reduce the risk of prostate and other forms of cancer
- decrease the incidence of type-2 diabetes
- inhibit the formation of peptic ulcers

Other benefits may include reduced risks of stroke, cataracts, anemia, and even the common cold.

In an article entitled *The Healing Power of Wine* (May 31, 2009), *Wine Spectator* concludes, "So the question is no longer whether moderate consumption of wine is healthy, but why and how."

Scientific attempts to understand the beneficial effects of wine have focused on chemicals known as polyphenols. Of these, resveratrol, a compound found in red wine, has received the most attention for its anti-aging effects. As Dr. Mehmet Oz writes in *You: The Owner's Manual,* resveratrol "seems to decrease the aging of the DNA in mitochondria—the cell's energy plant." Oz adds that this helps "reduce aging of the arteries and the immune system."

Dr. David Sinclair, co-author of a study of the potentially anti-aging effects of resveratrol published in the May 8, 2003, issue of the journal *Nature,* told reporters,"Not many people know about it yet, but those who do have almost invariably changed their drinking habits—that is, they drink more red wine."

A June 4, 2008, report in the *New York Times* proclaimed that "Red Wine May Slow Aging." The *Times* article reviewed the latest research by Dr. Sinclair and also included a discussion of the attempts by various pharmaceutical firms to develop anti-aging resveratrol capsules. (Sinclair recently sold his company, Sirtris —an organization focused on discovering and developing drugs with the potential to treat diseases associated with aging — to GlaxoSmithKline for $720 million.)

The *Times* story was sent to me by my friend Dr. Todd LePine, M.D., who serves as a consulting physician at Canyon Ranch, the renowned health resort. He included this delightful note: "The hell with the notion of an expensive pharmacologic pill to make us healthy. I'll take my medicine in a bottle with some good food, music, and friends!"

Dr. Le Pine's quip highlights another significant benefit of wine. It promotes relaxation, happiness, friendship, and gratitude. The benefits to emotional health go hand in hand with the physical benefits.

Wine isn't a panacea. There are a few medical conditions for which wine is contra-indicated. It's always a good idea to consult your physician before mixing wine with any medication. Drinking and driving is never a good idea. And overindulgence is dangerous.

When it comes to overindulgence, Ron White is an authority. In a classic moment from the hilarious "Blue Collar Comedy Tour," Larry the Cable Guy, Jeff Foxworthy, Bill Engvall and White are sitting at the counter of the Waffle House after a long night of shows and celebrations. With his customary cigar in hand and glass of Scotch nearby, White orders ham, eggs, grits, potatoes, waffles, and a few other dishes. The guys look on with amazement and Foxworthy asks, "Boy, how you gonna feel after you eat all that?" White grins and drawls back, "I didn't get to where I am today by thinking about how I'm gonna feel tomorrow!"

White is a living expression of Oscar Wilde's counsel, "Everything in moderation, especially moderation."

> *"The art in using wine is to produce the greatest possible quantity of present gladness, without any future depression."*
> —Thomas Walker (1784-1836) in *The Original*

Despite these amusing observations, moderation is the key to en-

joying and benefiting from most of life's gifts, especially wine. What
constitutes moderation? It differs based on weight, metabolism, age,
and gender. The general prescription is one glass per day for women
and two for men. (Why the gender difference? Besides the obvious
fact that women generally have lower body weight, they also produce
less, proportionate to body mass, of the alcohol-metabolizing enzyme
dehydrogenase. Thus a woman weighing, for example, 140 pounds will
process the alcohol in a glass of wine more slowly than a man of the
same weight.)

The Philosophy of Moderation

The idea of moderation as a key to the Good Life was developed by the Greek philosopher Epicurus (341–270 B.C.), who
also provided the philosophical basis for "the pursuit of happiness." Epicurus believed that happiness, moderation, and jus-
tice went hand -in- hand. He wrote, "It is impossible to live a
pleasant life without living wisely and honorably and justly, and
it is impossible to live wisely and honorably and justly without
living pleasantly."

Epicurus advises us to be mindful, asking ourselves: "What
will happen to me if that which this desire seeks is achieved,
and what if it is not?" He cautions, "No pleasure is a bad thing
in itself, but the things which produce certain pleasures entail
disturbances many times greater than the pleasures themselves." And he reminds us, "Be moderate in order to taste the
joys of life in abundance."

Unlike beer or hard liquor, wine has always been appreciated as the
beverage of moderation. Why? Because wine is designed to go with
food and to be consumed slowly so that it can be fully appreciated.
Drunkenness and alcoholism tend to be less common in societies like
Italy, Spain, and France where children grow up with wine at the table.

As the father of modern economics Adam Smith (1723—1790) noted in *The Wealth of Nations*, "The inhabitants of the wine countries are in general the soberest people in Europe."

In the wine country of southern Italy, archeologists discovered an ancient Roman winery with a Latin inscription that sums up the wisdom of moderation: "Who never drinks wine is a lamb, who drinks it properly is a lion, who drinks too much is a pig."

The Italians offer a wonderful toast: *cent'anni-* may you live for one hundred years. Wine may just help you make that so. Moderate, mindful enjoyment of wine can, as many physicians emphasize, help you "die young as late as possible."

PART 1

NAVIGATING THROUGH THE "WINE-DARK SEA"

"At sea a fellow comes out.
Salt water is like wine, in that respect."
—Herman Melville (1819-1891)
American novelist and poet

"No poem was ever written
by a drinker of water."
—Homer, (Eighth Century BC)
Greek epic poet

When I refer to the poetry of Homer I can usually count on someone wise-cracking: "Simpson?"

Actually, Homer Simpson offers a hilarious expression of the mindless approach to wine, in his classic observation: "Alcohol, the cause of and the solution to all the world's problems."

In the *Odyssey*, the original Homer refers to the sea as "wine-dark." His hero, Odysseus, confronts many challenging twists and turns on his journey. Here in Part 1, you'll learn how to navigate through another wine-dark sea as you master all the twists and turns of wine appreciation and etiquette. You will sail gracefully past the Scylla of Snobbery and the Charibdys of Corkage, and you'll become a hero to your guests as you order wonderful wine at a great price in a way that suits every situation. You'll discover how to see eye to eye with even the most Cycloptic sommelier. And you'll find new worlds of pleasure, enjoyment, and creative appreciation. Let's begin by exploring the art of tasting and enjoying wine, mindfully.

Sensazione-7:
The Art of Tasting

*"Wine is one of the most civilized things in the
world and one of the most natural things of the
world that has been brought to the greatest
perfection, and it offers a greater range for
enjoyment and appreciation than, possibly,
any other purely sensory thing."*
—Ernest Hemingway in *Death in the Afternoon*

When I'm leading an evening of wine-tasting and creative exploration, participants often ask me, "What's your favorite wine?"
My favorite answer is: "The one I'm drinking now."

The simple secret of appreciating wine or any other form of art is
to be fully present. But many of my friends and clients are so busy
working on creating a better future that they need help savoring the
moment. The great German poet Johann Wolfgang Von Goethe reflected on this phenomenon when he wrote, "One must ask children
and birds how cherries and strawberries taste."

How can we learn to taste and enjoy with the innocence and in-
stinctive delight of birds and children?

First, let go of the fear of embarrassment. The Sensazione-7 (*sensazione* is Leonardo's term for awakening your senses) approach to tasting is predicated on a simple but transformational question: "How do
you experience this wine?" **The beauty of this question is that it has
no wrong answers.** Freedom from the fear of being wrong allows us to
access our more intuitive, non-judgmental, right hemisphere.

As you learn to taste in this open, exploratory mode you'll also discover that it becomes easier to bring greater mindfulness to your senses. Being fully present while enjoying fine wine, beautiful music, or a glorious sunset makes a tremendous difference to the richness and clarity of the experience. Bringing greater awareness to the elements of your aesthetic experience is a simple and easy way to develop sensory intelligence.

In the Japanese tea ceremony, adepts invest years learning the nuances of pouring and appreciating a cup of tea. But you can learn the essentials of wine tasting in the time it takes to read the next few pages and you'll discover that this approach will deepen your enjoyment. If you are serving a rare, expensive wine then it's a waste not to apply this approach, and if you are drinking a well-made but relatively humble wine you'll find that these simple practices make the whole experience much richer.

There are seven simple elements to tasting and enjoying wine.

1: See
2: Swirl
3: Smell
4: Sip/Slurp
5: Swallow/Spit
6: Savor
7: Share

See

"Saper Vedere" (*Knowing How to See*).
— Leonardo da Vinci's motto

When you look at a glass of wine, what exactly are you looking for? First, look at the wine in your glass from above and then from a few different angles, especially from the side. It's helpful to view the wine against the background of a plain white tablecloth. Then, consider these two simple elements: color and clarity.

Color: White wines aren't white. They may be straw-colored, golden or yellow, perhaps with hues of the early morning or late afternoon sun. And red wines can be pinkish, mulberry, crimson, the color of Marilyn Monroe's puckered lips, or royal purple. In all cases, take time to enjoy the beauty of the wine's color and notice its intensity. Intense color often correlates with richness of flavor, but every now and then you'll be surprised when a very lightly colored wine bursts with yumminess. As fine white wines age, they tend to become darker in color, whereas older red wines become lighter. Older red wines also sometimes appear rust colored around the edge of the glass.

Clarity: When you plan to serve a fine wine, stand the bottle upright for at least a few hours first so that any sediment can settle to the bottom of the bottle. Older red wines often need decanting to help separate the sediment. Younger red wines often benefit from the aeration that decanting allows, and decanting is a delightful wine ritual. If your wine maintains a distinct haziness even after decanting then you may have a faulty bottle.

Sonic Wine, Pouring Secrets

Although sound isn't usually considered to be an essential element of wine appreciation the "pop" of the cork and the gurgle of the wine as it's poured into the glasses all add to the richness of the experience. As the Australian wine writer William S. Benwell mused, "The soft extractive note of an aged cork being withdrawn has the true sound of a man opening his heart."

And listening as you pour can help you fill the glasses evenly. How? Just listen for the same number of gurgles per glass.

❦ Swirl ❦

Swirling aerates your wine thereby liberating its bouquet and aroma. And it's fun.

The secret is to get the maximum swirl from the minimum motion. This takes a little practice. Hold the glass by the stem or base and move it in a tiny ellipse, using a subtle motion of your wrist. Or hold the glass still and then swirl your whole body like you were moving a hula hoop. Invite your drinking companions to stand up and practice the hula hoop swirl together. Accelerate the motion until the wine is flowing around the inside of your glass. When tasting Australian wines, swirl them in the opposite direction.

Check Out Those Legs!

Legs, also known as tears, are the rivulets that flow down the sides of your glass after swirling. More pronounced legs may indicate a more full-bodied, alcoholic wine, but don't necessarily correlate with quality.

❦ Smell ❦

You only need smell the wine
For vision to flame from each void,
Such flames from wine's aroma!
Imagine if you were the wine.
—Jallaludin Rumi (1207-1273) Sufi poet

Now plunge your nose deeply in the glass, close your eyes, and inhale.

In her marvelous book *The University Wine Course*, Professor Marian Baldy, Ph.D., emphasizes, "Our appreciation of wines is mainly due to their odors, and our sense of smell is our most important, sensitive and versatile sensory evaluation tool." We are capable of detecting more than ten thousand different aromas and can be trained, according to Dr. Baldy, to identify about one thousand. This makes wine appreciation easy since there are only about six hundred odorous compounds in wine. We can, for example, sniff out the compound that is responsible for the bell pepper aroma in a Cabernet Sauvignon at concentrations of one to five parts per *trillion*, which Baldy compares to, "sniffing out a one-cent error in your ten-billion-dollar checking account."

You can get the most pleasure from your wine by enjoying a few deep sniffs before sipping. Take your time appreciating the aroma (the specific smell of the grapes) and the bouquet (the *gestalt*, or whole experience of the smell). Experiment by angling your glass, or your head, to emphasize each nostril in turn, noticing differences in the nuances you perceive between left and right.

The most important point is to focus your full attention. As Robert Parker Jr. describes it, "When I put my nose in a glass, it's like tunnel vision. I move into another world, where everything around me is just gone, and every bit of mental energy is focused on that wine."

🍇 Sip/Swoosh 🍇

Remember when you were a kid and your mom told you to stop slurping your chocolate milk? Well, the good news is that you can now express your sophistication and savoir-faire by slurping and swooshing the world's finest wines. This is especially fun to do at a wine-tasting with your friends or colleagues, particularly when dining in an elegant restaurant. After sipping a petite mouthful of wine, purse your lips as though you were about to give your sweetheart a little kiss and then gently suck air into your mouth as you use your tongue to roll the wine around. (Lower your chin as you do this so the wine doesn't drip down your throat and cause you to gag.) Keep the wine in your mouth for about four or five seconds. This warms the wine and releases more of its pleasurable elements. Slurping and swooshing the wine around your palate, while drawing in more air, makes the flavors of the wine more pronounced. And the slurping noises make it almost impossible to take yourself or the process too seriously.

A few elements to enhance your enjoyment and appreciation at this stage:

• Notice the very first impression of the wine in your palate. (But delay summary judgment until at least your third sip. The first sip begins to condition your palate to the experience of the wine. The second sip invites you to a fuller appreciation. By the third mindful sip you have entered into a real relationship with the wine).
• Note the texture (silky, velvety, chewy?), weight (light, medium, heavy?) and flavors (fruits, sweetness, vanilla?).
• Try exhaling through your nose as you swoosh the wine around your palate. This is often messy at first and can result in hilarious reverse snorting, but once you master it you'll find that the impressions of the wine are magnified.

🍇 Swallow/Spit 🍇

If you are "just tasting," and especially if you are sampling many wines, then, of course, you'll want to spit, preferably into some sort of appropriate receptacle.

But for full appreciation and enjoyment you will swallow.

Close your eyes when you swallow and focus on the flavors, aromas, and sensations. As you swallow, become of aware of the feelings in your whole body. The finest wines make every cell of your body hum with pleasure. Natalie MacLean, author of *Red, White, and Drunk All Over* describes her experience of swallowing a Brunello di Montalcino in a chapter she entitles, "The Making of a Wine Lover": "My second glass tasted like a sigh at the end of a long day: a gathering in and a letting go. I felt the fingers of alcoholic warmth relax the muscles at the back of my jaw and curl under my ears. The wine flushed warmth up into my cheeks, down through my shoulders, and across my thighs. My mind was as calm as a black ocean. The wine gently stirred the silt of memories on the bottom, helping me recall childhood moments of wordless abandon."

As Natalie MacLean's rhapsody suggests, the pure experience of sensory awareness can transport us to a rebirth of our childlike innocence. Full presence in the moment calms the mind, opens the heart, and deepens our pleasure.

Commit to the Spit

In addition to slurping and swooshing, wine tasting also allows grown-ups to spit in public, politely. The art is to do so without dribbling on your shirt or spraying another taster. After swooshing the wine around your palate, position it in the front of your mouth, ready for expulsion. Align with your target and expel the wine in a direct, steady stream. If you hold back you're more likely to dribble or spray, so: Commit to the spit.

In his classic *The Vineyards of France*, J. M. Scott counsels that your spitting must be as "bold and emphatic as an exclamation mark." Of course, if you have a prominent gap between your top front teeth, then you are probably a natural expert.

🍇 Savor 🍇

"A scent of flowers, radiance, and heat, are distilled here to a fiery, yellow liquid. This is rapture. This is relief."
—Virginia Woolf (1882-1941) English novelist, describing her experience of savoring a sip of wine.

Kevin Zraly, author of the *Windows on the World Complete Wine Course*, guides his students to spend at least sixty seconds savoring after swallowing. Why? Because the best part of a fine wine is revealed *after* you swallow it.

Don't rush to take another sip or a bite of food until the full experience has played out in your palate. Take time to enjoy the lingering flavors and sensations.

A bad wine will finish like Thomas Hobbes's (1588 -1679) description of an unenlightened human life: "nasty, brutish and short."

The finest wines, like the greatest works of art, reveal different nuances and subtleties with every sip. Great wines are like the best symphony orchestras, with all the instruments playing in perfect harmony. A balanced, harmonious wine yields a seamless experience of pleasure rather than jarring notes of acidity and alcohol or cloying tones of fruit and sweetness. Great wines can continue to reveal exquisite, delicious qualities in your palate for more than two minutes after swallowing. Of course, simple wines can also be very enjoyable, preparing your palate perfectly for the next big bite of pizza.

❦ Share ❦

"The pleasure of wine consists only partly in itself; the good talk
that is inseparable from a wine dinner is even more important
than the wines that are being served. Never bring up your
better bottles if you are entertaining a man who cannot talk."
—Maurice Healy (1887-1943),
in *Claret and the White Wines of Bordeaux*

Sharing your experience of the wine brings the pleasure to another level.

Hugh Johnson, author of *Vintage: The Story of Wine,* explains,

"Wine is the pleasantest subject in the world to discuss. All its associations are with occasions when people are at their best: with relaxation, contentment, leisurely meals, and the free flow of ideas." The most important thing to remember in sharing your experience is that there are no wrong answers to the questions, "How do you experience this wine? What are your impressions?"

Master of Wine Jancis Robinson shares a story of her initiation into the highest levels of wine description when she attended her first professional wine-tasting event: "Hugh Johnson was there, and the editor of *Decanter* magazine, and, horror of horrors, we all had to sit round a table and opine. I carefully watched what they did (much slurping and spitting) and copied them, while keeping very quiet indeed. But after listening to them all trying to describe the same wines and doing it with completely different and sometimes contradictory words, I realized that applying words to wine is a complete free-for-all."

Robinson adds, "There are no rights or wrongs in wine appreciation and no absolutes when it comes to tasting terms, so the opinion of the novice is every bit as valuable as that of the expert. In fact I often find that novice tasters are much better at coming up with the perfect word to describe a wine flavor than us professionals who used up our tasting vocabulary years ago."

As Robinson suggests, innocence and openness often lead to the most lively and compelling descriptions. Wine description really is a free-for-all. The freer you feel to share your experience of the wine in imaginative, multi-sensory terms, the more you will enjoy and remember.

Multi-Sensory, Right-Brain Wine Appreciation

"Wine evokes memories, especially scents of childhood because as kids we took time to experience the world around us. Most adults tend to shut this process down, but playing with analogical thinking and poetry is a wonderful way to reawaken this openness."
—Craig Williams

The framework of right and wrong, or accurate and inaccurate, is useful when we are dealing with matters of fact. This is the realm of the more analytical left hemisphere. Left-brained wine appreciation focuses on questions with definitive answers such as:
- Where is the wine from?
- What's the varietal?
- How old are the vines?
- What were the conditions in the vintage?
- What was the yield per acre, or hectare?
- When were the grapes harvested?
- What's the alcohol level?
- How was the wine aged? (Steel? French, American or Slovenian oak barrels?)
- How long was it aged?
- How much does it cost?

Some folks are interested to know about differences in winemaking techniques and clonal cultivation strategies, but for many people that's a bit too much like work. Of course, this type of information can enhance appreciation and enjoyment, just as it can be useful to understand the influences of Beethoven on Brahms. But the real magic comes when we open our senses and intuitive minds to music, wine, and life.

Alfred North Whitehead (1861-1947), English mathematician

and philosopher explains:

> *"You may learn all about the sun, all about the atmosphere,*
> *all about the rotation of the earth,*
> *and still miss the radiance of the sunset."*

Neuroscientists estimate that your unconscious, non-verbal intuitive database outweighs your conscious, verbal awareness by more than 100,000 to 1. You can access your vast intuitive power, magnify your appreciation, and liberate your creativity by posing open-ended questions. The beauty of these questions is that they encourage you to stop worrying about getting the right answer so that you can put your full attention on enjoyment. As you let go of the fear of being wrong or saying something silly and bring your full attention to the experience of the wine, you enter the realm of multi-sensory, right-hemisphere appreciation. This attitude to appreciation focuses on an innocent, playful, and metaphoric expression of your pure sensory experience and the impressions evoked. As Jose Ortega y Gasset (1883-1955), Spanish philosopher, notes:

> *"The metaphor is perhaps one of man's most fruitful potentialities.*
> *Its efficacy verges on magic, and it seems a tool for creation which*
> *God forgot inside one of His creatures when He made him."*

So experiment with musing on questions such as these:
- How do I experience this wine?
- How does it make me feel? What emotions does it evoke?
- What images, associations, colors, or memories does it inspire?
- What music does it bring to mind? (Jazz? Rock? Soul? Country? Classical? Opera?)
- If this wine were a painting, who would be the artist? (A cave painter? Rothko? O'Keefe? Raphael? Pollock? Monet? Hals? daVinci?)
- If this wine had a shape, what would it be? (Angular? Flat? Dimensional? Conical? Circular? Spiral?)

- If this wine could dance, what dance would it do? (Waltz? Hip-hop? Foxtrot? Ballet? Tango? The Twist? Hula?)
- If this wine was a car, what would it be? (Mustang? Mercedes? Prius? Hummer? Magnum? Mini Cooper? Lamborghini?)
- If this wine was a kiss from a celebrity, who would it be? (Scarlett Johansson? Amy Winehouse? Charlotte Rampling? Pamela Anderson? Danica Patrick? Margaux Hemingway?)
- If this wine were a movie, who would be its director? (Fellini? Fassbinder? Coppola? Bergman? Meyer? Hitchcock? Truffaut?)

At first these types of questions can seem "off-the-wall" but, after the second glass of wine, everyone embraces them enthusiastically.

What to Wear with What You Drink

Leslie Sbrocco, author of *Wine for Women*, explores the delightful question: "If this wine were clothing, what would it be?" She compares different grapes to various outfits and accessories:

Sauvignon Blanc	Crisp white blouse
Merlot	Soft cashmere sweater
Syrah	Stylish red leather bag
Cabernet Sauvignon	A knockout business suit
Riesling	A comfortable, figure-enhancing bra
Chardonnay	Basic black
Sangiovese	Chic Italian high heels
Pinot Noir	An elegant, classy, and glamorous silk dress
Zinfandel	Black leather trousers

Soc It to Me!

One of Socrates' friends asked the Oracle at Delphi, "Who is the wisest man in Athens?" The Oracle proclaimed, "Socrates." When Socrates was informed of this, he responded by attempting to prove that the Oracle was mistaken. Seeking to discover who was truly wise, he questioned others about the meaning of truth, goodness, and beauty. Most of the people he approached were unable to offer well-reasoned answers; instead they clung to prejudices and preconceptions or they pretended to know something that they did not know, rather than admit their ignorance. Socrates realized that perhaps the Oracle was right after all, since he knew, and was willing to accept, what he did not know.

The famous Socratic Method is a process of questioning designed to help students overcome their prejudices and preconceptions and discover the truth for themselves. Socrates, and his great student Plato, believed that all knowledge worth knowing was already present within the student.

When it comes to appreciating fine wine, a lighthearted version of the Socratic approach invites us to a deeper, freer and more authentic experience of this sensational libation. The secret is to approach wine enjoyment, like Socrates would, in an open, questing, and curious manner.

When describing a wine most folks, beginners and experts alike, make statements about the wine that are declarative: "This wine is." But, of course, what they are really saying is, "My experience of this wine is." You needn't actually use that phrase; just remember not to commit the fundamental philosophical error of confusing subjective experience with objective reality.

If you've ever been to a formal wine-tasting, you've probably heard someone describe a wine by saying something definitive and oracular, like this actual expert description of a Sauvignon Blanc from New Zealand: "moderate intensity on the nose with scents of gooseberry, wild hedgerow and a touch of chalk, it reveals a good sense of minerality; the palate well-balanced with kiwi fruit and ripe green apples, leading toward an understated finish."

What's the most fruitful way to approach someone else's wine description? Use it to enhance your own process of inquiry and appreciation.

In the example above you can get the most from the expert's description by taking a Socratic approach. So as you enjoy the wine, you might ask:

- How would I describe the intensity?
- Do I smell:
  Gooseberries? (This is a ubiquitous wine-geek descriptor for Sauvignon Blanc, despite the fact that most Americans have never smelled an actual gooseberry. Although they come in different shapes and colors, unripe gooseberries taste like sour white grapes. Ripe ones are harder to find, and taste like a combination of pineapple, strawberry and Muscat grapes. But, if you are a professional wine writer, it's considered bad form to describe a wine with references to grapes, hence the prevalence of the g-word.)
  Wild hedgerow? (Versus cultivated hedgerow?)
  Chalk? (Blackboard? White Cliffs of Dover?)
- What other words come to mind to describe the aromas?
- Do I taste: Kiwi fruit? Ripe green apple?
- What other words come to mind to describe the tastes?
- How long does the finish last? Is there another word that states it more clearly for me than "understated"?

Consider treating all wine descriptions, expert or not, as provocations for deeper questioning, exploration, and enjoyment. An additional benefit of this approach is that you may become more curious about the aromas, tastes, and all the sensory impressions in your world; bringing more mindfulness to your next gooseberry, hedgerow, or green apple, for example, as well as your next New Zealand Sauvignon Blanc.

Chris Coad, creator of the website Compleatwinegeek.com, describes the beneficial effects of this open, exploratory approach as he began to embrace his passion for wine tasting: "One of the most delightful aspects of my new hobby was that I soon discovered that simply trying to pay close attention to the messages my senses were sending me paid unlooked-for dividends in terms of really tasting food and smelling all kinds of things that had previously gone by unnoticed (not necessarily a blessing in Manhattan, but hey, you take the good with the bad).

I have always loved to cook, and I noticed that I was becoming much more aware of the interplay of spices and the texture and color of food, and found that many foods seemed to taste better when complemented by the right vino. This, of course, is hardly an original idea, but there is no truth quite like an old truth that you discover for yourself."

Comparative Appreciation

When most folks are first asked to describe wine, they will often say something like:

"I don't know, it tastes like wine," or, "It seems pretty grapey to me."

These descriptions are fine, but a bit limiting in terms of facilitating depth of appreciation, recall and enjoyment. As you get outside of the box by playing with a Socratic approach to multi-sensory right-brain description, you can then take everything to another level of pleasure and understanding by practicing comparative appreciation.

So what's better than listening to one beautiful version of Beethoven's Symphony Number 5? Listening to two beautiful renditions. What's better than enjoying one exquisite single vineyard Barolo from Maestro Roberto Voerzio? Comparing two, from different single vineyards.

The pleasure, delight, and depth of appreciation isn't just enhanced arithmetically by having more music or wine— it evolves exponentially.

When we compare music, wine, or any other art form with an open mind and heart and a sense of pure curiosity, we experience with greater depth. We remember better. We discern nuances and distinctions that might otherwise escape our attention. We nurture our sensory intelligence. And we find inspiration.

After comparing two wonderful wines from southern France, a father of two daughters wrote:

Wine is like daughters

One is with darker complexion
Tart, sassy
A little kick
Always the last remark

The other
Bright
Sparkling
Effervescent
Always a spark

Different
Unique
But each special in her own way
Each reminding me that life is worth sipping
Slowly.

Comparative appreciation is a wonderful way to stimulate your imagination and bring more joie to your vivre. When you taste a flight of wines or listen to multiple versions of a musical composition, your mind will naturally attune to the differences and similarities between them. As you make these distinctions you tend to notice and appreciate greater subtleties in the wine or the music. The comparative process happens effortlessly, deepening your memories, pleasure, and eventually your connoisseurship.

As you apply the Sensazione-7 approach to tasting and experiment with a Socratic, multi-sensory, right-brain approach to comparative appreciation, you will get more value out of every wine you drink. But how do you find the best value wines to compare and describe? How do you deal gracefully with sommeliers and snobs? Are there times when red wine is perfect with fish? When should you send wine back? Is it appropriate to sniff the cork? Read on, and you will soon know how to sail smoothly through the Wine-dark sea.

Mastering Wine-Lists, Sommeliers, Snobs, Corks, and Etiquette

"Wine has shown me matters in their true perspective, and has, as though by the touch of a magic wand, reduced great disasters to small inconveniences. Wine has lit up for me the pages of literature, and revealed in life romance lurking in the commonplace."
—Alfred Duff Cooper (1890 –1954),
British poet and diplomat

I go to Disneyworld a few times every year. It's not because of the rides at the Magic Kingdom, but rather, it's a common destination for corporate conferences and therefore keynote speeches. On my last visit, I gave a keynote on the topic "Innovation: Doing More with Less." Afterward, my client took me to a fancy steakhouse and handed me the wine list. It had many impressive, but dramatically over-priced selections. Most of the bottles were marked up at least three times their fair retail value. There were plenty of wines from big-name producers but mostly from off vintages. It was a minefield, and a challenge to drink more for less. The good news is there was one fine wine that was fairly priced (double retail—perhaps they'd made a mistake?) and an ideal accompaniment to the other guests and the food they'd ordered (steak!). My client loved it and was particularly impressed by the value.

Although I champion the role of the right-hemisphere—non-judgmental, intuitive, imaginative— as the key to profound appreciation and pure enjoyment, the left hemisphere is necessary to set the stage.

Obtaining fine wine at a reasonable price calls for a logical strategy. Whether you are dining out with friends, ordering wine on a hot date, or hosting a dinner for an important business associate, it's great to feel confident and poised when the wine-list is presented to your table. As wine becomes a more integral part of our culture it makes sense to be well versed in the appropriate protocol. This can be especially crucial in a business or professional situation, but the knowledge and *savoir faire* you need is basically the same whatever the context.

Ten years ago, the *Wall Street Journal* observed: "Wine at business meals is a skirmish in a boardroom war, played out on a linen table cloth. Your handling of wine, whether ordering it or just drinking it, matters more than you think to your colleagues. Sometimes people see your comfort or expertise with wine not as a comment on your knowledge, but on your character."

Just as people will judge your character based on the quality of your tie or shoes, they will also make assessments based on your wine knowledge or lack thereof. Wearing cheap shoes and a tie that doesn't match or ordering an over-priced wine that clashes with what your client, or your date, has just ordered for dinner can both cause embarrassment. It's good to know how to avoid embarrassment and triumph in skirmishes, but mastering wine protocol offers many more benefits. Knowing your way around the world of wine can make meals, and deals, far more pleasurable and can contribute to developing rapport with your date, clients, colleagues, and other associates. It can sometimes be the catalyst for closing a sale or beginning a romance.

My first great romance was kindled during a candlelit dinner in a dorm room as we enjoyed a bottle of Bolla Valpolicella. The wine helped create an ambiance that inspired a sweet, soulful rapport, transforming a potentially awkward moment into an exquisite one. (And 38 years later we are still friends; and, as our friendship has evolved over the years, so has the winemaking at Bolla.)

In a professional context, my experience with wine spans thirty years and many different cultures. My first senior executive seminar was held in Vevey, Switzerland, in 1979. I was twenty-seven, and most of the participants were considerably older. Each night after class they ordered magnums of wine and tried to get me drunk. In Japan, in the early '80s, clients proffered endless waves of sake, wine, Scotch, beer, and cognac as a prelude to mandatory karaoke performances. During four months of seminars in Sweden in 1984, I experienced the ritual of the "Skål." Dating back to the time of the Vikings, the Swedish toasting custom involves raising one's glass and looking the person(s) with whom you are drinking in the eye as you both say "Skål." After you sip, you keep your glass elevated and make eye contact again before putting your glass down. This ritual evolved as a way to keep an eye on your companion to ensure that he wouldn't cut your head off between sips.

Traditionally, only a senior person can initiate the "Skål," but the junior person must reciprocate. Here's where it gets tricky: The junior person must wait at least one full minute before returning the "Skål," but no more than three minutes. The time begins from the moment the senior puts down his glass, and the junior must never put his glass down before the senior. Although I was the seminar leader I was also the youngest and therefore the most junior. I did quite well in responding to the first three or four "Skåls," but after being toasted by the tenth member of the team, everything got a bit hazy.

When I returned to the United States after my adventure in Sweden, a more sober attitude seemed to prevail. Despite a few experiences of the soon-to-be vestigial three-martini lunch, most conferences and social events were decidedly un-Dionysian, usually beginning with a perfunctory cocktail hour and then some mediocre-to-bad wine with dinner.

Now many more folks are becoming interested in wine and want to experience more. The general level of wine lists and service in the United States has improved and will probably continue to do so. Wineries in California, Washington, Oregon, and other states are making wine at the highest level of quality. In 2008, for the first time ever, Americans drank more wine in total than Italians. As James Laube, senior editor of the *Wine Spectator* observes, for too many years the culture of wine in America, "veered between 'wino' and 'wine snob,'" symbolized by cheap domestic plonk or the veneer of imported sophistication." Now, he emphasizes, "Our tastes set standards around the world."

The standards of good taste in the world of wine are easy to learn. Knowing the essentials of wine etiquette has become at least as important as knowing how to dress for success. Let's consider the vital aspects with a view toward making the most of every wine encounter.

Here are a few fundamental principles:

• **Be prepared.**

It's much easier to ensure a positive experience if you know where you are dining, what's on the wine list, and something about the preferences of the other diners. Once you know the venue, you can check out the wine list online or have it faxed to you.

• **It's more important to match the wine to the people and the occasion than to the food.**

It's wonderful to know about the fine points of pairing food and wine— we will cover this later in this section — but the most important consideration is discovering what will best suit the preferences and tastes of your fellow diners.

• **Humility is the soul of confidence.**

You needn't ever pretend to know more than you actually do. And, in the world of wine, there is always so much more to know. But, at the same time, never allow yourself to succumb to the feeling of intimidation. With good humor and common sense you can handle anything.

- **Know your tolerance for alcohol and don't exceed it.**
  In Japan, it's fine to get totally wasted at a business dinner. Nothing you say or do will be held against you the next day. In the United States and most other places the opposite is true; you are judged on your ability to maintain your composure while drinking.

- **Whenever possible, choose a wine-friendly venue.**
  Ordering wine is much easier in a wine-friendly restaurant. Some characteristics of wine-friendly restaurants are:
  - The wine list is well chosen and the mark-up isn't more than 100 percent of retail.
  - The wine list is up-to-date. Vintages are listed accurately.
  - The wine list has many selections that were specifically chosen to complement the style of food served.
  - The sommelier (aka "The Wine Steward" or "Wine Director") knows the wines and is sincerely focused on making you happy with your choice.
  - Appropriate glassware is provided. (Flutes for bubbly, and a clear, stem crystal with a bowl big enough for swirling for everything else.)
  - The sommelier presents the bottle you've ordered for your approval and opens it in front of you. He pours you a small amount so that you can be sure that the wine isn't faulty. If appropriate, he offers to decant the wine for you.
  - The wine is served in moderate pours (approximately 3 to 5 oz.) and glasses aren't "topped up" after every sip. (When too much wine is poured in your glass you can't swirl it without spilling.)

- When a new bottle is brought to the table, new glassware is provided. The assessment ritual is repeated.
- Wine-friendly restaurants also welcome BYO (if state and local laws allow it — some states and counties are more wine-friendly than others) and offer a reasonable corkage fee.

Over the last thirty years, friends, clients, and colleagues have asked all kinds of wine-related questions. Here are some of the most common and important.

What do I do if I find myself at a restaurant that isn't wine-friendly? For example, there's no sommelier and the wines are listed without vintages?

Ask your server, " Who knows the most about wine?" If there's a good wine list but no sommelier there's usually someone who knows about the wines. Sometimes the manger, owner, or even the chef will come to help you.

When the vintages aren't listed ask your server for a pad of paper and a pen. Write down the bin numbers of the wines you are interested in and ask him to go to the cellar and check the vintages for you.

If your server seems poised to overfill and "top-up" your glasses do not hesitate to say, "Thanks very much, I will pour the wine." And ask for new glasses if they aren't presented when a new bottle is brought to the table.

If the glassware is insufficient, ask your server or the manager to please find some better glasses. They often have a few better quality glasses set aside for customers who specially request them.

Is glassware really that important?

If you have the chance to hear one of the world's great mezzo-so-pranos, like Susan Graham, Anne-Sophie von Otter, or Deborah Do-manski (my wife), you wouldn't ask her to sing in a basement. A beautiful voice should be heard in a venue with excellent acoustics. And a fine wine should be served in an appropriate glass. If you're drinking 2-Buck Chuck then a styrofoam cup will do, but if the wine is fine you need appropriate glassware.

When I first heard about the idea that specialized glassware could highlight the nuances of different wines I was skeptical. But then I discovered that fine red Burgundies really do taste better in a Star Trek thermos and Alsatian Rieslings show best in a Scooby-Do mug. Kidding aside, although it's possible to enjoy a fine wine in an ordinary glass, it *is* better in a great glass. A great glass optimizes the sensory profile of the wine. It provides a better feeling in your hand, greater ease of swirling, and enhanced clarity of color, aromas and flavor. Test this yourself by experimenting with a comparative tasting: Start with a fine wine. Pour some in a paper cup, a juice glass, a standard issue wine glass, and the appropriate Riedel glass. You don't have to be a connoisseur to discover that the wine displays different characteristics in each vessel.

If fine glassware isn't easily available, then just relax and make the most of the situation by bringing extra attention to savoring the wine. (You can, if necessary, sometimes bring your own glasses to a restaurant, and fine wine glasses make wonderful presents for all your friends who aspire to learn about wine).

> *What are the responsibilities of the sommelier, and do I need to tip?*

The word *sommelier* comes from the Medieval Latin root *summare*, which means "to calculate a sum." A sommelier's job is, ultimately, to sell you as much wine as possible. Thirty years ago the average sommelier was an intimidating figure haunting fancy French restaurants with what seemed like a shiny ashtray dangling around his neck. (This accoutrement is known as a "tastevin"— its reflective surface was useful for highlighting a wine's color and clarity in a dark cellar.) In the last few decades restaurateurs have learned that the sum of wine sold will be greater if the sommelier is helpful and supportive rather than supercilious and condescending. Contemporary sommeliers tend to be passionate and knowledgeable about wine in general and their lists in particular. They are involved in every facet of a restaurant's wine program and supervise all aspects of the wine service. Today, most sommeliers are focused on understanding the taste of their customers and satisfying them so that they will want to return to the restaurant and order more wine. Sommeliers usually earn a percentage of wine sales and don't necessarily expect a tip but will happily accept one. (Sommeliers are a much more diverse group than they used to be. In the last decade or so many women have embraced the profession –*sommeliere*— and there are many more young people with a much greater variety of ethnic backgrounds. Salud!)

How can I work effectively with the sommelier?

Ask questions. Point to two wines that you've had before or two that you are considering and say something like: "I'm trying to decide between these, unless there's something you think we might like even more." This lets the sommelier know the type of wines you like and your price range.

You may also ask: "What do you think are the best values on the list?" "What are your favorite wines on the list?" and " What do you recommend with the food we are planning to order?"

Then, watch the sommelier's body language and facial expression as he responds. You can usually determine the level of genuine enthusiasm for a given recommendation by paying careful attention. You must discern whether the recommendation is based on a sensitive and caring assessment of your desires or an overstock of a well-hyped but not particularly special wine.

At a recent dinner at the magnificent Spanish restaurant Taberna del'Albardero in Washington, D.C., I spied two wonderful wines offered at a reasonable price. I asked the *sumiller* (Spanish for sommelier),

" The Numanthia and Pintia seem to be great values, unless there's something you think we'd like even more?" He smiled and said, "San Ramon." His upbeat body language and shining eyes conveyed his sincerity and pride, and the wine he recommended was 10 percent less than the other wines. It was fabulous.

> *What should I do when the sommelier presents the bottle?*

When the wine is presented always inspect the bottle. Notice if there is any leakage around the capsule (the foil, plastic, or wax enveloping the cork and part of the neck of the bottle) or if the wine doesn't fill the bottle to its neck. (The space between the wine and the top of the bottle is called *ullage*.) These are signs that the wine is probably flawed. Read the label carefully and ensure that it is the wine you ordered in the correct vintage. If not, send it back, except in the unlikely circumstance that you are mistakenly brought a better vintage than the one you ordered.

A well-heeled client recently took me out to dinner and asked me to order the wine. I know he loves Bordeaux and that his price comfort level is no more than $100 per bottle. I ordered the 2005 Chateau Duhart Milon Rothschild, listed at $95, a great value for this junior sibling of the first growth Lafite Rothschild. After a relatively long time the sommelier returned with a bottle of the 2002. He apologized for the discrepancy in vintage. I thanked him and asked for another look at the list. The 2003 Branaire Ducru was listed for $125, also a good price, but above my client's ceiling. I asked the sommelier, "We had our hearts set on the 2005 Duhart. I see you have the 2003 Branaire. Would it be possible to make an adjustment in our favor?" He graciously offered it to us for $95. The moral of the story is that when you are brought an incorrect and inferior vintage of the wine you've ordered, you have an excellent opportunity to give the sommelier or server the chance to make amends.

? *What should I do when the sommelier presents the cork?*

Craig Williams shares this true story of a quirky cork assessment: "One of my friends went to a family get-together at a prestigious restaurant in the Monterey area of California. They select a wine, the sommelier opens it and presents the cork on a small silver plate, which he places next to my friend's mother-in-law. She picks it up, gives it a quizzical once-over, and proceeds to take a bite out of the cork!"

Although cork chomping is somewhat unusual, most diners will have witnessed dramatic incidents of cork sniffing, a la Pepé le Pew. This can be fun and may impress Penelope Pussycat, but it isn't necessary, as its much better to just smell the wine in the glass.

As more fine wines utilize artificial cork and screwtops, this ritual will probably fade away. In the meantime, simply assess that the cork isn't rotten and notice its quality. (Every now and then you will find that the cork crumbles as it's removed. But as long as the very bottom of the cork has maintained its integrity the wine can still be sound.) The best cork is tight and smooth but malleable under the pressure of your fingers. If you like, you can roll it around in your hand to enjoy the texture as your server pours the wine.

"Twisted but not screwed"

Dr. William Gardner is the founder and chief technology officer of Gardner Technologies and the inventor of the Meta Cork. An emeritus Professor from the College of Engineering at the University of California at Davis, Gardner took on the challenge of finding a functional and aesthetically pleasing alternative to cork. He developed a hard plastic capsule with a threaded inner surface, and a matching plastic threaded cap that is screwed into the cork during the bottling process. So users can just twist off the capsule and push out the cork without a corkscrew.

Gardner explains, "I was convinced there was a better solution than the corkscrew and the less-than-perfect screw-caps currently used on wines. After observing so many people struggling to open a bottle of wine and having to cope with broken corks stuck in the bottle, cork crumbs in the wine, and corks pushed into the wine, as well as negative image problems with screw-caps and their defective or easily damaged seals, I knew this was a problem waiting for a solution and was a challenge I wanted to take on."

Gardner's innovative product is marketed with the slogan "Twisted but not screwed."

When should I send wine back?

If the wine is corked (contaminated with a chemical known as TCA), cooked (ruined by over exposure to heat) or oxidized (stale). The best sommeliers will notice this before serving the wine. They know right away from the smell out of the bottle. If you suspect that the wine is tainted, if it has no aroma at all or if it smells like wet cardboard, a damp basement, vinegar, or excrement (not too be confused with the seductive "barnyard" aromas from some fine burgundies and other great wines), then summon the sommelier and say, "There seems to be something wrong with this wine, what do you think?" Most sommeliers will graciously agree and whisk the offending bottle away before returning with the list. If you encounter resistance then feel free to meet it with insistence: "This wine is flawed, please remove it from the table and from my bill." The opportunity to sample the wine presupposes your right to reject it.

If the wine truly is flawed then the distributor will refund the restaurant's cost. And if you are wrong in your assessment, you needn't worry, as the sommelier will probably sell the wine by the glass for an even bigger profit.

Sometimes a wine seems "off" but the cause isn't in the bottle, rather it's the improperly rinsed wine glasses. You may want to sniff your glass while its still empty to be sure its not redolent of Cascade.

> *When is it appropriate to bring my own bottle to a restaurant?*

When you have a special bottle that isn't on the wine-list. Always call ahead to the restaurant and confirm that it's okay to bring your wine. It's also a good idea to check on the amount of the "corkage fee" (the fee the restaurant charges for each bottle you bring, usually between $15-$25). If you also order something from the list the corkage fee will sometimes be waived, especially if you offer your server and/or sommelier a taste of the wine you brought.

> *If I'm the host how do I order wine that will make all my guests happy?*

Ordering champagne to start usually makes everyone happy. In the United States most folks think of champagne as a wine of celebration, reserved for New Year's Eve or Formula One racing triumphs; ordering it to begin the meal sets a celebratory, festive tone that promotes rapport and good fellowship. (It's best, however, not to spray it on your guests.)

As you enjoy the bubbly, you might ask your guests, "What types of wine do you like?" "What's the best wine you've had recently?" Calibrate everyone's level of knowledge and experience, based on their answers, and then look for something that will extend their potential for enjoyment without overstretching it. When dining with people who have greater wine knowledge and experience, elicit their recommendations. As you assess the tastes and preferences of all the guests, you also want to discover their choices for the main course, so you can find compatible matches. Sometimes, its best to order a different wine by the glass for each guest based on stated preferences. Other times a spontaneously arranged comparative tasting is the way to go. Magnums (the equivalent of two regular size bottles) are fun with larger groups. Pinot Noir is a good choice to complement both meat and fish dishes. Sometimes you will want to go with a "sure thing" and order wines that you know are consistently excellent. On other occasions you will want to go into unknown territory to find something new and exciting. In addition to calibrating tastes and preferences it's useful to assess the appropriate level of risk-taking for a given situation.

Use your creativity and intuition in harmony with common sense and careful analysis of the situation. Consider the nature of the occasion. The appropriate wines for a company picnic will differ from those for a night out with friends, a new product launch celebration, a family reunion, or a high-profile client dinner.

On special occasions, elicit your guest's preferences before the event and arrange to have her favorite wine decanted and waiting at the table upon arrival.

> *What's the appropriate response when the host asks me to order the wine?*

Diogenes (412—323 B.C.), the ancient Greek philosopher and founder of Cynicism, stated, "I like best the wine drunk at the cost of others." It's nice to be treated by a friend, suitor, supplier, salesman, or client; but ordering the wine as a guest requires extra consideration.

As you learn more about wine you will find yourself in this situation frequently. Always strive to find value for the host while endeavoring to help everyone present enjoy the best possible wine. If you are not sure of your host's budget, then make recommendations of the best wines on the list at three different price levels. Describe the wines and then point to the list so that the host can see the prices. Ask,"I've narrowed it down to these three; which one sounds best to you?"

> *What about occasions when the wine is pre-ordered and mediocre, such as "Rubber Chicken" dinners?*

Fund-raising events, conventions, conferences, and even board/senior executive dinners are rarely graced with fine wine. If you want something better you can ask for a wine list, order something wonderful, and pay for it separately, as long as you include your whole table. The legendary author of *The Physiology of Taste*, Jean Anthelme Brilliat-Savarin (1775-1826), opined, "A dinner without fine wine is like a day without sunshine." You can, of course, smuggle your own sunshine into these events. Offer some to everyone at the table and make many new friends.

> *How can I be sure to get good wine service?*

The key to getting good service is the same as getting good support in any area of life. Always remember that we teach people how to treat us. We teach them how to treat us by how we treat them. Kindness, respect, and humor bring out the best in everyone. Expect the best from people, without an attitude of entitlement, and you will usually get it.

> *How do I deal with wine snobs?*

The word "snob" comes from the Latin phrase *sine nobilitate* meaning "without nobility." A *snob* is someone who "patronizes or ignores anyone they perceive as inferior in social position, education, or taste" (Oxford English Dictionary).

Like the world of classical music and fine art, wine seems to attract plenty of snobs. Those who devote years to the study of finer things can easily slip into identifying themselves with the objects of their study. Although immersion in life's finer gifts, such as, for example, the music of Mozart, the painting of Leonardo or the first growths

You're not actually going to have that Chateau L'Effete with fried chicken are you?

of Bordeaux, does indeed provide an ennobling influence, these aesthetically uplifting delights are, all too often, perverted by the grasping of the ego.

Most snobs are harmless. They will usually ignore you although they may manage a condescending expression if you dare to express an opinion in their presence, especially if you demonstrate enthusiasm. In the wine world, the worst snobs are what Gary Vaynerchuck, founder of WineLibrary.com, calls "wine bullies." He defines a "wine bully" as "One who uses their knowledge of wine to abuse others." Wine bullies go out of their way to put others down for their choices and expressions of taste. Classic wine bully comments include:

"You didn't really drink the wine when it was that young, did you? Why, that's infanticide."

"You're not actually going to have that Chateau L'Effete with fried chicken, are you?"

"You prefer lush, new-world wines? How infantile."

Along with snobs and bullies, the wine world also has its share of reactionaries or "reverse snobs." They look down on anyone or anything with an aristocratic background. They like to think of themselves as down-to-earth and unpretentious, but these positive attributes are, in the reverse snob, also tainted by the ego. Reverse snobs delight in denigrating wines that are sought after and critically acclaimed. They eschew any ritual or accoutrement associated with tradition and refinement and wouldn't be seen using a decanter or fine glassware. They insist on wine without a pedigree, preferably from a jug, box, or a screwtop bottle. Among the most egregious reverse snobs are amateurs who make their own dreadful wine and insist that you drink it.

While studying in London in 1975, I met my first reverse wine snob at a dinner party. He insisted that we all drink the wine that he made from the vines he had planted in his garden. He went on interminably about his cultivation and vinification process and proclaimed repeatedly that his wine was superior to the "overpriced rubbish from across the channel." The British are very polite and long-suffering, so everyone did their best to humor him, but when he asked loudly, "Why, do you realize that this wine came from the grapes grown right outside this window?" one wag couldn't resist and responded, "Hmmm, doesn't travel well, does it."

The best policy with all the foibles described above is, first, to examine yourself to be sure that the ego isn't driving your relationship to wine and those with whom you share it. If you experience the paternalism of the snob, the contempt of the bully, or the reactionary practices of the reverse snob, do your best to meet them all with compassion and humor.

What about wine-related headaches?

Some folks get headaches from listening to wine snobs drone on endlessly about *terroir* and malolactic fermentation, but many people also get headaches from actually drinking wine, especially red, and often assume, incorrectly, that sulfites are the culprit. Used by winemakers worldwide to preserve wine, sulfites are only a problem for the very small percentage of people who are allergic to them. (The warning on wine bottles "contains sulfites" is intended to protect the 1 percent of the population who are allergic to sulfites. The most common symptom of sulfite allergy is an asthmatic-like difficulty in breathing)

If you do suffer from wine-related headaches here are a few things to consider:

Quantity—The most common cause of a wine-related headache is drinking too much. Experiment to discover the amount you can drink without discomfort. Many people find that they are fine with one or two glasses and the headache only becomes an issue after the third glass. (It's also advisable to drink two full glasses of water for every glass of wine you enjoy. The alcohol in wine can cause dehydration and dehydration can cause headaches.)

Type—Before generalizing and proclaiming, "I get headaches from red wine," try different types of wine, noting your relative sensitivity. Some people get headaches from Cabernet Sauvignon, for example, and not from Pinot Noir. You may also discover that the frequency and severity of the problem declines in direct proportion to the quality of the wine you drink. Chuckie Shaw probably causes many more headaches than Louis Latour.

Timing—Many people find that drinking wine on its own, as a cocktail or aperitif, results in more headaches than enjoying the wine with food.

Charles Camille Heidsieck (1820-1871) aka "Champagne

Charlie" helped introduce bubbly to the United States. His proposed remedy for hangovers and headaches was, not surprisingly for so passionate a salesman, a glass of champagne. As he wrote:

> What matter if to bed I go
> Dull head and muddied thick
> A glass in the morning
> Sets me right very quick

Do you have any advice for ordering wine when I'm dining alone?

Wine is the catalyst for conviviality, and its pleasures multiply when shared. But if you are a road warrior then you will frequently dine alone and wine can enhance the experience significantly. When you dine solo you can bring your full attention to savoring your wine. You may even be inspired to write a poem, like this one by the great Chinese poet Li Po (701-762):

Drinking Alone Beneath the Moon

> A pot of wine among the flowers,
> I drink alone, no kith or kin near.
> I raise my cup to invite the moon to join me,
> It and my shadow make a party of three.
> Alas the moon is unconcerned about drinking,
> And my shadow merely follows me around.
>
> Briefly I cavort with the moon and my shadow,
> Pleasure must be sought while it is spring.
> I sing and the moon goes back and forth,
> I dance and my shadow falls at random.
> While sober we seek pleasure in fellowship,

When drunk we go each our own way
Then let us pledge a friendship without human ties
And meet again at the far end of the Milky Way.

The good news for solo wine aficionados is that many restaurants are expanding their options for wines by the glass and increasing their inventory of half-bottles. A few tips to make the most of the singular wine experience:

- Ask for tastes: If you plan to have a wine by the glass you can ask your server for a taste of a few of the wines you are considering. Besides helping you make a more informed choice you will enjoy a mini comparative tasting without incurring additional expense.
- Ask them to split a bottle: Despite the trend to provide better selection by the glass and half-bottle, many establishments remain behind the curve in this noble endeavor. So if there's a wine on the list that you desire but is only available in a full bottle, it can't hurt to ask the sommelier or a manager if they will sell you half. (they can then sell the remainder by the glass). This works about 25 percent of the time.
- Ask if there's anything special available by the glass that isn't on the list: Sometimes there's an open bottle of something wonderful because someone else has followed the previous suggestion, or, because, earlier in the evening, a sound wine was rejected by another diner.
- Order a whole bottle and share it with the staff or other diners. Not only will you make new friends, but others will often reciprocate; just be ready for a party.

My budget is very limited. Why should I bother learning about wines that I can probably never afford?

Wine Spectator magazine recently featured a list of top-rated Burgundies from the 2006 vintage. The average cost of the wines was over $200 a bottle. That's way out of my price range. But it's still fun to learn about them. As British poet Robert Browning (1812-1889) reminds us "a man's reach should exceed his grasp, or what's a heaven for?"

And learning about heavenly, expensive wines can yield benefits other than just pure inspiration. If you organize a group of four friends you can split the cost of an expensive bottle and make it affordable. This is a great way to experience the finest wines of the world and a wonderful means of bonding with your friends.

Although most in-store wine tastings feature inexpensive wines, every now and then, they open something special. My local supermarket offers a free wine tasting every Saturday, usually featuring wines under $20, but last week they were pouring the Domaine Tempier Bandol *La Tourtine*, a killer wine from Provence that retails for more than $75.

And a local wine store held a tasting a few weeks ago that cost just $10 and included generous pours of the full range of wines from Napa Valley's Heitz winery including the legendary Martha's Vineyard, retailing for $175 a bottle (the $10 was credited toward any purchase in the store).

It's good to recognize great free wine and enjoy it. And your knowledge can also pay off when you spot pricing anomalies in stores or on restaurant wine lists. My wife and I went away for a mini-vacation recently. On our first night, we dined at the bar of a highly-rated restaurant, and, after perusing the wine list, discovered something that seemed too good to be true: The 2006 Beaux Freres Pinot Noir from Oregon for $70! I asked our server if he actually had the wine at that price (average *retail* price is $85). He returned with a bottle and said that he checked it in the computer and it was supposed to be $195 but that he would sell it to us for the price on the list. Without missing a beat my wife said, "Can you please sell us another one at the same price for tomorrow night?" (This is part of why I married her!)

Moreover, as you learn about fine wines, you mobilize the psychological "Law of Attraction" in your favor. The "Law of Attraction" posits that you will draw into your life—for better or worse—the things and experiences that you focus upon. After years of visualizing the experience of legendary bottles, I've attracted Chateau Petrus, Domaine Romanee Conti, Krug Clos des Mesnil and Angelo Gaja wines to my palate, from generous folks with fabulous wine collections who were just waiting to share their treasures with someone ready to appreciate them. (You can, of course, also apply this law to attracting more wealth so you can afford more expensive wines). Cheers!

Can you give me some ideas on themes for wine tasting?

Winston Churchill commented, "Even pudding [British for *dessert*] needs a theme." You can make every wine experience more memorable by organizing your choices around a theme.

Finding great value is always a compelling theme. We recently invited a group of friends to our home for a wine dinner. We served three red wines and asked our guests to guess the similarities between them (besides all being red). Someone guessed, incorrectly, that they were all the same varietal (i.e., grape variety). Another guest suggested that all the wines were from the same region, but that wasn't the case. Finally, someone said 'Well, one thing they all seem to have in common is that they are all very good." At which point the secret was revealed. They were all very good: Each wine was rated more than 91 points by Robert Parker and cost under $13.

Another popular theme is to compare wines at different price points. At an event at a friend's home we enjoyed three Champagnes from Veuve Cliquot: Veuve Cliquot NV, the 1990 Vintage, and the 1990 Grande Dame. (The vintage Veuve is almost twice as expensive as the famous orange label non-vintage, and the Grande Dame is three times the price.) Everyone loved all the wines and discovered that to get full value for the more expensive wines it was essential to pay very careful attention to the subtleties and nuances.

At a retreat for the principals of an accounting firm, we enjoyed three Merlot-based wines from Falesco in Umbria: Vitiano ($8), the Merlot ($14), and Montiano ($45). When preferences were revealed, participants discovered the "cheap dates" in the firm.

Other delightful themes to enjoy:

• The same fine wine from different vintages: Compare, for example, the 2001, 2003, and 2004 versions of the marvelous Northern Rhone Cornas from Auguste Clape. (This is known as a vertical tasting.)

• The same grape, from the same region and year, from different producers: Compare three great expressions of Brunello di Montalcino from 2001, such as Ciacci Piccolomini, Fuligni, and Il Poggione. (This is a horizontal tasting. You can also, of course, compare the same grape and year from different regions.)

If there are wineries in your state or region then it's fun to compare your best local wines with one another and against similar wines from other regions. For example, we recently held a tasting of top New Mexico Pinot Noirs and then compared them with Pinots from Oregon.

You can also compare regular bottlings with reserve wines and note the differences you experience. The reserve is usually aged longer and represents the best grapes of the vintage and, of course, it usually costs more. Is it worth it?

It's also illuminating to compare different styles of wine, for example, an unoaked Chardonnay and one that is heavily oaked. Experiment with a tasting of wines that are all produced biodynamically. Find wines that are featured in books or movies that you enjoy, and taste while reading passages or viewing. For example, read passages from Ian Fleming's James Bond novels while enjoying the champagnes that 007 prefers (Bollinger, Veuve Cliquot, Krug, Taittinger, and Dom Perignon), or watch *Sideways* while enjoying a comparative tasting of Pinot Noir or Merlot.

Matching Wine and Music

Exploring the pairing of wine and music makes a lively party theme. Ask your wine and music-loving friends to bring a bottle and the music that they feel accompanies it best. Listen, drink, and compare notes.

What's the right order to serve different wines?

Whenever you are serving multiple wines, it's useful to understand the natural progression of taste. Generally, as a meal progresses, it's best to move from the light, simple, and dry toward the heavier, more complex, and sweet. If you go the other way around it creates a sensory anti-climax that usually disappoints. The exception is when you are at a noisy, busy place that makes it challenging to pay attention to the subtleties of the wines. In this circumstance, its often best to serve the finest wine first to make a vivid "primacy effect" (the psychological term for the tendency for people to remember what comes first) impression on your guests.

How do I know when a wine is ready to drink?

The vast majority of wine produced around the world is meant to be consumed upon release. Many of the finest wines, however, do require further aging to reach their peak. But for how long? Kevin Zraly advises that a wine is ready to drink, "when all the components are in balance to your particular taste." The only way to know if the components are in balance for your particular taste is to drink a lot of wine at different stages of its evolution.

Ageworthy wines tend to shed obvious fruitiness and gain complexity over the years. Bold, tannic red wines become softer and more approachable. Fine white wines, like, for example, a top-quality chardonnay, can develop an exquisite caramelized, crème brulee quality with age. The storage conditions, type of grape, region, and wine-making style all affect the rate of aging. A properly stored, traditionally styled Barolo or Brunello di Montalcino from a great vintage will require at least ten years in the bottle to be ready to drink, while a top-level Oregon Pinot Noir from a superb year will be ready in half that time. Of course, these judgments are all subjective. As you drink and pay attention you'll discover whether you prefer to err on the side of wine that is young or old.

If you drink a wine when it's too young, you can enjoy imagining the qualities that will emerge as it matures and mellows. If you drink a wine when it's too old you can speculate on its former glory. Ideally, you'll find what's *just right* for you. The good news is that once a wine reaches maturity, it will usually remain in its optimal state for a while—in other words, it will *plateau* before it slowly begins to fade. (Legendary Master of Wine Clive Coates posits a Law of Maturity — a wine will remain on a plateau of peak drinkability for as long as it took to reach maturity. That is, if a wine reaches its optimal state after ten years of aging, then it will remain at its best for another ten years before it begins to decline.)

Fortunately, most professional reviewers will give you their best estimate of a wine's aging potential. You can also ask your sommelier or wine merchant, and you can consult the label or the website of the winery for the winemaker's recommendation as to the ideal timing for your enjoyment.

> *"[One notes] its gracious withdrawal from perfection, keeping a hint of its former majesty as it hovers between oblivion and the divine untergang [German for downfall] of infinite recession."*
> —Stephen Potter, author of *One-Upmanship*, describing a wine that's too old.

Does the size of the bottle affect the aging process?

Wine ages faster in smaller bottles. If you love vintage port or Sauternes and you don't want to wait thirty or forty years for it to be ready to drink, then you may want to buy it by the half bottle. On the other hand, connouisseurs generally agree that the magnum is the perfect size for the optimal aging of the finest red wines.

How long can I keep a bottle of wine after opening, and what's the best way to preserve it?

Once you've opened a bottle of wine the inflow of oxygen begins the process of oxidation. In its early stages this process is known as aeration or *breathing,* and it can make the positive qualities of the wine more accessible. As oxidation continues, however, the wine eventually degrades and becomes undrinkable.

So you can preserve your wine by limiting the oxidation process. Most wine stores offer a few different gadgets, including pumps to draw the oxygen out of the bottle, and other systems that create a cushion of inert gas, thereby displacing the oxygen. The simplest and least expensive method is to keep a supply of different size plastic or glass bottles (empty spring water bottles and half-bottles and splits of wine are ideal). Pour your unconsumed wine into a smaller bottle and fill it to the top, then cork or cap the bottle and *voila´,* you are keeping the oxygen out and the freshness in.

You can also help maintain the freshness by placing the wine you are saving in a cool dark place. Some wines will surprise you by lasting for many days after opening, and others will fade overnight. Sauternes, port, and other sweet wines will tend to last longer, but not forever. On average, good wine stays good for about two or three days after being opened when it's stored properly.

> *I've heard about gadgets that accelerate the aging of wine. Do they work?*

The simplest way to simulate the effects of aging is to decant your wine and let it breathe for a few hours. (For a wonderful lesson in the value of decanting watch episode 18 of Wine Library TV with Gary Vaynerchuk: http://tv.winelibrary.com).

If you can't get around to decanting your wine a few hours before you intend to drink it then you may want to explore a few of the gadgets on the market for accelerating wine maturity. Most notable among these is the Vinturi Essential Wine Aerator. Recognized as one of the 15 revolutionary inventions of 2007 by Entrepreneur.com, the Vinturi is a clear, elegant funnel through which you pour your wine into a glass or decanter. Although the physics behind its operation are complex — the patent-pending device is based on the principles of fluid dynamics first propounded by Daniel Bernoulli (1700 -1782)—its use is simple; and tasters in an independent, double blind test conducted by the Vinquiry laboratory in California identified the wine that had passed through the Vinturi as "higher in overall flavor, intensity, and mouthfeel … and overall aroma intensity … more true to type and of higher quality." For under $40 it's a great wine-geek conversation piece.

Other gadgets including The Perfect Sommelier ® and The Wine Clip ® apply principles of electro-magnetism to accelerate the movement of your wine's molecules to simulate the aging process. These devices have been endorsed by luminaries such as Anthony Dias Blue and Master of Wine Mary Ewing-Mulligan. They also cost about 40 dollars and offer another way to amuse your cork dork friends.

The Vinturi, TPS and Wine Clip are based on principles of physics—fluid dynamics and electro-magnetism, respectively. The Clef du Vin, developed by sommelier Franck Thomas and oenologist Laurent Zanon, is based on principles of chemistry: using a special metal alloy to serve as a catalyst of a wine's process of oxidation. The inventors claim that the device—it looks like a small kidney-shaped pocket knife—is calibrated precisely so that each second in which the tip is dipped into your wine will simulate the effect of a year of aging (i.e. one second of dipping equals the effect of one year, 2 seconds, two years, etc.)

Does it work? Well, it does seem to change the aroma and flavor of the wine. But does it do so systematically, in the manner claimed? Some users say that they get the same effect from dipping a polished copper penny in their wine, and the penny is $99.99 less that the CdV. Gary Vaynerchuk compares the effect of the Clef du Vin to a "kid who who has skipped a couple of grades in school"—the child may be advanced intellectually but can't keep up emotionally. (Check out Vaynerchuk's Clef du Vin comparative tasting on Wine Library TV: Episode 274.)

How does temperature affect wine?

It's best not to drink if you have a fever. But seriously, be aware of the season, ambient temperature, and relative humidity as you choose your wine. It's hard to focus on a heavy red wine when it's 95 degrees and humid, and a steely, cold white isn't usually the right choice on a frigid winter evening. And the temperature of the wine itself is important—most whites are served too cold and most reds are served too warm. Don't hesitate to ask a sommelier or server to either provide an ice bucket or to wait and allow the wine to warm to a more appropriate serving temperature.

Serving Temperature

One mega-brewery advertises their product as "the coldest tasting beer." Cold, of course, isn't a taste, it's a reference to temperature. Lower temperatures suppress aromas and flavors and higher temperatures highlight them. But if served too warm, wines lose their edge and become flabby.

It's best to suit the serving temperature to your own taste, but here's a little tip to guide you: 20-30 minutes in or out. If you pull a bottle of a fine white out of the refrigerator it's a good idea to wait about 20-30 minutes before drinking it, and since "room temperature" in the United States averages 72 degrees — too warm for all reds — don't hesitate to pop your red in the refrigerator or ice bucket for 20-30 minutes before enjoying it.

Type of Wine	Recommended serving temperature (°F)
• Champagne and other sparklers	40-48
• Sauvignon Blanc and other crisp whites	45-52
• Chardonnay, Sauternes, and Riesling	50-58
• Rose, Beaujolais	54-60
• Pinot Noir, Grenache	57-65
• Cabernet Sauvignon, Merlot, Nebbiolo, Tempranillo, Shiraz, Zinfandel	60-65

Can you give me some guidance on how to propose a toast?

The ability to offer an appropriate toast is an important element in your repertoire of social skills. Whether you are toasting at a wedding celebration, birthday party, or anniversary dinner or giving a eulogy, toasting a client at a business dinner, or giving out awards for the most evocative poetry at a wine-tasting event, there are a few simple guidelines that can make the experience a delight for all involved:

- **The Host Initiates:** It is the responsibility of the host or Master of Ceremonies to initiate the toasting. If there's a special "guest of honor" then the host or M.C. should toast that person first. (If it seems that the host isn't going to propose the toast, it's appropriate to discreetly ask for the host's blessing before doing so yourself.)

- **Stand and Deliver:** Unless you are in small informal group, it's appropriate to stand when proposing a toast.
- **One Toast at a Time:** Avoid the temptation to piggy-back return toasts onto the original toast. Allow each toast to stand alone.
- **A Toast Is a Presentation:** The best toasts follow some simple principles of effective presentation. These principles are:
- **Be Prepared:** Anticipate the circumstances where it may be appropriate for you to offer a toast and be prepared. The best extemporaneous speakers are those who have planned for spontaneity. As Mark Twain (1835-1910), quipped, "It usually takes me more than three weeks to prepare a good impromptu speech."
- **Focus on the Audience and the Context:** Know where you are and to whom you are speaking. "Customize" your remarks to the circumstances.
- **Be Authentic:** In Hollywood and Washington, D.C., everyone knows that sincerity is the key to success, and that once you learn how to fake that you've got it made. Of course, it's much better to actually be sincere. A heartfelt expression of acknowledgement is always well received and appreciated.
- **Your Body Language Is at Least as Important as Your Words.** Be upright and open. Smile. Make eye contact with the person you are toasting and with everyone present. As William Shakespeare (1564-1616), advised "Suit the action to the word, the word to the action."
- **Be Brief:** Always leave them wanting more, rather than the alternative. Apply the KISS principle (Keep It Simple, Speaker). "Brevity is the soul of wit," so in the words of Franklin D. Roosevelt (1882-1945): "Be sincere, be brief, be seated." And always finish on a high note with a positive, uplifting tone.
- **Practice Toasting at Toastmasters:** As they proclaim on their

website, "No, we don't make toasters!" Since 1924, Toastmasters International has offered a simple and effective forum for people to develop excellent presentation skills. With more than 11,000 clubs in 92 countries, this non-profit organization provides a supportive framework for participants to become comfortable and competent at delivering a prepared speech or impromptu remarks.

A Brief History of Toasting

In Shakespeare's *Merry Wives of Windsor*, the wine-loving Falstaff demands, "put toast in't" when he asks for a jug of his favorite libation. Falstaff's request was an expression of a practice begun by the ancient Romans of dropping a piece of charred bread into wine of dubious quality. The Romans discovered that charcoal tempered the unpleasant acidity of many common wines. Eventually, the Latin word *tostus* meaning "roasted" or "charred," originally applied to the process of making wine more palatable, came to refer to the process of drinking the wine.

Although the term *toast* comes from the Romans, the practice of raising one's glass before drinking originated in ancient Greece. Poisoning was a common method for dispatching one's enemies, and a considerate Greek host reassured his guests by pouring all the wine from a shared vessel that he sampled first. Having thus demonstrated the safety of the wine he would then fill each cup from the common vessel and raise his cup while inviting everyone to drink in good health. The custom was refined with the additional ritual of clinking cups together. The clinking often caused at least a few drops of wine to slosh from cup to cup, providing additional assurance that the drink was safe. The raising of glasses together thus became a symbol of trust and an affirmation of friendship.
Cheers!

TIPPSY:
A Wine-Buying Strategy

"Shalt then be thine, that nectar rare
Which brightens hope and drowns dull care.
Come taste my wine, but ere thou try it,
Remember, friend, that thou must buy it."
—Horace (65 – 8, B.C.)
Roman poet in *The Odes*

I make a good living, but I'm not too focused on material things. I live in a comfortable, modest home. I own a sports car, but I've had it for six years and will probably keep it for a few more. I can't think of anything that money buys that gets me particularly excited, except for wine! My greatest motivation to earn more money is to be able to afford the wines I want, to share them freely with my friends, and to raise the standard of my house wines. I've been hunting down wine values for three decades, and I'm passionate about it. I swear it tastes better when you get a good deal. In this chapter I will share with you everything I've learned about how to buy wine and find value.

Do you work in an H.A.C.? (High Acronym Culture) Acronyms are useful because they make it easier to remember and communicate. TIPPSY is an acronym to help you remember the most important considerations in buying wine. The TIPPSY approach includes everything you need to know to make intelligent buying decisions for your own pleasure or in social and business circumstances. As you apply it, you will discover great values as you deepen your appreciation and enjoyment.

T - Type: What type of wine do you like?
I - Inventory: Is it available?
P - Producer: How good is the producer?
P -Price: Is it a fair price?
S - Score: Can you find a reliable rating?
Y - Year (Vintage): What is the quality of the year?

> *"Life is too short to drink bad wine."*
> —Wine cellar graffiti
>
> Actually, life is too short to drink mediocre or even good wine when you can drink very good and sometimes great wine for reasonable prices.

❦ Type ❦

What type of wine do you like? That's the first and most important thing to consider when deciding what to buy. The way to discover what you like is simply to drink and pay attention.

As you explore different types of wines you'll discover that your tastes change over time. Developing your palate for wine is similar to developing your ear for music. At first the distinctions are very simple. Red or white? Jazz or classical? Dry or sweet? Orchestral or chamber?

If you decide, for example, that you like classical music and you want to learn more, you begin to listen and pay attention. You start to make distinctions between composers. You become aware of the differences between Mozart, Bach, and Beethoven. Then you listen to Brahms, Chopin, Handel, etc. As you listen and pay attention you develop preferences for particular composers and the way their music is expressed by various conductors, orchestras, and soloists. Eventually, you can discern the sound of different instruments in an orchestra and the way they all play together.

If you decide you like wine and want to learn more, you begin to drink and pay attention. You make distinctions between the different types of grapes. You start to be able to tell the difference between a Cabernet Sauvignon, a Pinot Noir and a Merlot; and you notice the way they are interpreted in different regions and by various producers. Just as a classical music lover learns to appreciate the interpretation of the notes by different artists, you begin to become aware of the subtle nuances of aroma and taste in the types of wine you love.

If you've never listened to opera and you hear the winner of Britain's equivalent of American Idol, Paul Potts, sing Puccini's "Nessun Dorma" for the first time, there's a good chance you'll enjoy it. Just like tasting your first oaky, buttery Chardonnay. Then, if you hear Andrea Bocelli sing "Con Te Partiro," it's another revelation, like your first juicy, peppery Zinfandel. Some people stop at this point and think they know opera and wine. But, if you are wise, you listen to Luciano Pavarotti, Placido Domingo, and Dmitri Hvorostovsky and you try Bordeaux, Burgundy, and Barolo. And, then you go on to explore marvelous voices that are still relatively unknown like Aaron Pegram, Simon O'Neill, and Weston Hurt and you explore wines from Languedoc-Roussillon in France, the Mosel-Saar-Ruhr region in Germany, and the Douro Valley in Portugal.

You can accelerate the development of greater clarity about what you like by focusing on a particular type of wine for a set period of time. Let's say you want to explore Merlot. Make your next month the merry month of Merlot. Explore various manifestations of the grape from different regions of the world at various price points. If possible, aim to taste the very best Merlots from around the world so you can benchmark for excellence. As the poet Johann Wolfgang Von Goethe reminds us, "One cannot develop taste from what is of average quality but only from the very best." You can further deepen your appreciation, enjoyment, and recall by keeping a notebook to record your impressions, preferences, and descriptions. Then, the next month, choose another type of wine, perhaps Chardonnay, Sauvignon Blanc, Riesling, Cabernet Sauvignon, Shiraz or Pinot Noir, and rinse and repeat.

Another delightful way to approach this exploration is by focusing on the wines of countries, or particular regions, that you want to learn about. You can spend a week, a month, or a year, for example, immersing yourself in the cuisine, culture, and language of a region that fascinates you as you enjoy the wines from that part of the world. Using this approach you can bring Tuscany, Provence or Ribera del Duero into your home, and you can use the money you save on airfare to buy the best wines.

Just like learning about music, appreciating wine offers a lifetime of excitement, discovery, and delight. There are exquisite classics that you can always enjoy and an endless variety of new types to explore.

The Elements of Style: Best Cellars

You can accelerate your appreciation for the type of wine you enjoy by learning more about the styles you like best. In their wonderful book, *Wine Style: Using Your Senses to Explore and Enjoy Wine*, Mary Ewing-Mulligan and Ed McCarthy divide both reds and whites into four distinct stylistic categories. These categories help you to approach ordering and buying wine through words that relate to your experience of the wine. Although most wine stores and restaurants categorize wine by grape variety or region there is an increasing trend to list them by style. Mulligan and McCarthy offer the following basic stylistic categories for whites and reds:

WHITES:
•**Fresh and Unoaked**
•**Earthy**
•**Aromatic**
•**Rich and Oaky**

REDS:
• **Mild-Mannered and Subtle**
• **Soft and Fruity**
• **Fresh and Spicy**
• **Intense and Powerful**

Another approach to buying by style, rather than grape type or geographic origin, was pioneered by Josh Wesson, winner of the competition for the best Sommelier in America in 1984. In 1996 he launched Best Cellars, a wine store with a "style-oriented" approach, employing simple categories with corresponding color codes and icons to help customers find the wines they like. In 1997, *Food & Wine* magazine named Wesson the Retail Wine Innovator of the Year for his work in developing Best Cellars. Although the company was sold to A & P in 2007 the concept continues to thrive with nine stores in five states and an online outlet: www.bestcellars.com

❦ Inventory ❦

Once you know the type of wine that you like you will want to consider this simple but very important question: Can I get it? There are many highly desirable wines of the world that are, more or less, unavailable. To paraphrase Woody Allen's description of his favorite adult movie: It's filled with images of people better looking than you will ever see, doing amazing things that you will never get to do. Similarly, you may never see or have the opportunity to taste many of the fine, critically acclaimed wines that you read about in various publications because they never make it to the shelf of your local wine store. These wines are often snapped up by restaurant buyers or pre-sold on mailing lists.

Yes, you can sign up for winery waiting lists for special wines and go to auctions to acquire the rare and wonderful, but common sense dictates that it's better to choose wine that you can find without the oenological equivalent of an FBI manhunt. The best way to buy wine is to find a good local wine store—or two, so you can comparison shop— and establish a rapport with the sales staff. Browsing through the aisles, handling the bottles, asking questions, and discussing experiences with a real person and, of course, enjoying free in-store tastings, are all advantages of buying wine "live" in a local store. And you can take the bottle(s) home and drink it the same day. Moreover, as you get to know your local wine merchant he or she will begin to let you know about the arrival of "highly allocated" wines that never make it onto the shelves.

Beware the Phantom Inventory

In a restaurant that doesn't invite BYO, you are limited to whatever the current inventory happens to be. Many wine lists are replete with desirable selections that aren't in stock. So when you are dining out you want to make the best choice from what's actually available. Since the phenomenon of phantom inventory is common, it's a good idea to be prepared with a second or third choice.

Searching for wines on the Internet can also be fun, and it gives you access to a much greater inventory, but there are some hazards. Many merchants advertising on the web are just plain unreliable. Shipping charges and handling practices can vary dramatically. You may find that your wine takes months to arrive and, in the meantime, you are subject to an onslaught of e-mails touting all sorts of undesirable plonk. Many wine websites are cumbersome, cluttered, and clueless. And be aware that some states do not allow wine to be shipped to their residents. You may spend an hour browsing a site and placing an order for the wine you desire only to discover that it can't be shipped to you.

Dorothy J. Gaither and John Brecher, the brilliant wine columnists of the *Wall Street Journal,* recently published their wish-list for what every online wine merchants' website ought to have, including:

- Reliable real-time inventory, with images of the actual bottle for sale, including updated, accurate vintage and pricing information.
- Clearly stated shipping policies—so you don't waste your time if it's illegal for them to ship wine to your state. It's also useful to know how the wine is being shipped, exactly when it will arrive (you don't want your case of fine wine sitting on your porch for seven hours in 85-degree weather), and how much it will cost.
- Accurate reviews from major wine publications, rather than proprietor propaganda.
- Specific contact information for the person with whom you are doing business, including their geographical location. As Gaither and Brecher write, "We like to know who's getting our credit card number."

The Best of Vineyards: Wine Storage Tips

The best way to ensure a healthy inventory of fine wine is to keep your own supply. Lord Byron (1788-1824) explains:

> *An English autumn, though it hath no vines,*
> *Blushing with Bacchant coronals along*
> *The paths o'er which the far festoon entwines*
> *The red grape in the sunny lands of song.*
> *Hath yet purchased choice of choicest wines;*
> *The claret light, and the Madeira strong.*

> *If Britain mourn her bleakness, we can tell her,*
> *The very best of vineyards is the cellar.*

A few simple points to remember:

- Rest your bottles sideways to keep the cork moist.
- Storage temperature should be cool and consistent: 55 degrees Fahrenheit is ideal; 70 is the max. Most importantly, avoid extreme temperature fluctuations.
- Sustained exposure to bright light, vibration (from a nearby washing machine or refrigerator) and lack of humidity (minimum 60 percent humidity will keep your cork from drying out) can ruin your precious bottles.
- If you can't create a wine cellar, find a dark closet, cabinet, or room with a relatively cool, consistent temperature.

🍷 Producer 🍷

As you discover the types of wine you like you'll begin to learn about the best producers. Returning to our music analogy, a great producer is like a great conductor. The best conductors possess a profound knowledge of the score and a passionate love of the music. They will audition and select only the very finest musicians, and they will demand the highest standard of play. Moreover, the very best conductors are true to the music written by the composer— they don't distort, add, or attempt to "improve" on a masterpiece by Mozart or Beethoven.

If you want to enjoy a great symphony or opera you can be sure it will be wonderful if it's conducted by Leonard Bernstein, James Levine, Sir George Solti, Lorin Maazel, Sir Charles MacKerras, Zubin Mehta, or Herbert von Karajan.

Similarly, a great producer has a profound knowledge of wine making and a passionate love for wine. He will conduct a rigorous selection process and choose only the finest grapes. The very best producers are true to the land and the grapes they grow—they don't manipulate and twist their wines to be something different than they are.

So if you love Nebbiolo, for example, you can be confident that it will be wonderful if it's produced by Aldo Conterno, Bruno Giacosa, Roberto Voerzio, Vietti, Bartolo Mascarello, Bruno Cerretto or Domenico Clerico.

The finest producers provide consistent high quality and value at every price point. They bring you the best available wine every year. If the grapes are compromised by poor conditions in a given year the best producers will not put them in the bottle.

Discovering the producers you like and trust will help you to make good decisions about what to buy. You can complement your knowledge of the best producers by learning about the best importers and distributors. The best importers and distributors are like impresarios. The best impresario will only produce a concert with the best conductor. And the best importers and distributors will only feature the best producers. Among the best of the best are:

Leonardo LoCascio, Marc DeGrazia, Neal Rosenthal, Neil Empson, Eric Solomon, Terry Thiese, Martine Saunier, Robert Kacher, Fran Kysela, Michael Skurnik, Kermit Lynch, Becky Wasserman, Jorge Ordonez, Dan Philips, Weygandt-Metzler, Monika Caha, Manny Berk, and Vias

So if you see these names on a bottle – often on the back label— you know that the wine is probably fine.

Taste the Silence

- Beauty is more important than impact.
- Harmony is more important than intensity.
- The whole of any wine must always be more than the sum of its parts.
- Distinctiveness is more important than conventional prettiness.

- Soul is more important than anything, and soul is expressed as a trinity of family, soil, and artisanality.
- Lots of wines, many of them good wines let you taste the noise, but only the best let you taste the silence.
—"Manifesto" of importer Terry Thiese, explaining his criteria for choosing the wines and producers he represents.

🍇 Price 🍇

"There is no money, among that which I have spent since I began to earn my living of the expenditure of which I am less ashamed, or which gave me better value in return."
—George Saintsbury (1845-1933), British author and critic, on buying wine in *Notes on a Cellar-Book*

Every now and then a generous host says these magic words at the beginning of dinner: "Please order whatever you think is the absolute best wine— price isn't a consideration." Ah, sweet music!

But even when a magnanimous benefactor offers carte blanche, the instinct for value must remain undimmed. And in the vast majority of situations, price *is* an important consideration. If you are buying wine for your own pleasure you want to get the highest quality wine at the best possible price. If you are in a business context, an attunement to value sends a strong positive message.

Value is the relationship of price to quality in context. If the context is closing a big deal, then Dom Perignon and Opus One may be considered superb values, if your client perceives them as highly desirable.

Just like any other commodity, wine is subject to the laws of supply and demand. Some grapes, like Pinot Noir and Nebbiolo, for example, are much harder to cultivate and therefore are usually pricier. You can assess your bottle of wine, at every price point, against other comparably priced bottles. Check the comparables and seek the incomparable.

Wine, like other commodities, is often marketed and hyped to raise the perception of its relative value. Many global brands spend more on the marketing and the advertising than they do on making the wine. Sometimes a beautiful bottle and snazzy label correlate with high quality, and other times they don't. How can you tell the difference?

As you drink and pay attention over the years, you can benchmark levels of pleasure at various price points and improve your ability to assess value. While you're cultivating that ability, it's extremely useful to find a critic whose palate and integrity you trust. Most critical guides let you know the price you can expect to pay for a wine and will give you an assessment of relative value.

A great way to begin is to read Robert Parker's reports on the "Wine Bargains of the Year" (You can access this by subscribing to *The Wine Advocate* or by joining eRobertparker.com). Comb through his reviews and highlight those with the most appealing descriptions and highest ratings. Check the inventory at your local wine shops and buy as many of the wines as you can find. Then, over the next few days invite your friends over for a series of comparative tastings. You are likely to find at least one amazing discovery that you can translate into your "house wine."

Amazing Wine Values

Over the last few decades I've held many value-oriented comparative wine tastings for my friends and clients. The wines listed below are those that have shown well year after year. (Some vintages are better than others, but one of my criteria for inclusion on this list is consistent quality.) They are all relatively easy to find, and they are all no more than $20 per bottle (prices listed are the best I've paid for these wines in the past year). These bottles compare favorably with wines that are priced two or three times more. Wines marked "HW" are those that I have bought by the case and served as house wine:

SPARKLING WINE:

Segura Viudas NV "Aria" Estate Brut Cava ($10)—Spain
Gruet: All of their sparkling wines are exceptional, especially their Rosé ($12)—New Mexico (HW)
Riondo Veneto Prosecco ($13)—Italy
Domaine Ste. Michelle Blanc de Blancs ($15)
—Washington State
Gloria Ferrer Brut ($16)—California
Lucien Albrecht "Cremant d'Alsace Blanc de Blanc – Brut"($18)
—France
Roederer Estate Anderson Valley Brut ($19)—California
Schramsberg "Mirabelle" North Coast Rosé ($19)
—California

WHITE WINE:

Domaine de Pouy Vin de Pays des Côtes de Gasgogne ($9)
—France
Columbia Crest Chardonnay "Grand Estate" ($11)
—Washington State (HW)
Pascal Toso Chardonnay ($12)—Argentina
Leasingham Riesling Clare Valley Magnus ($12)—Australia
Pierre Sparr Alsace Riesling ($13)—France
Huber "Hugo" Niederösterreich Grüner Veltliner ($13)
—Austria
Beringer Alluvium Proprietary White ($14)—California
Yalumba Chardonnay Wild Ferment ($15)—Australia
Kim Crawford Sauvignon Blanc ($15)—New Zealand (HW)
Godeval Vina Godeval ($15)—Spain (HW)

Colome Torrontes ($16) — Argentina
Torbreck Woodcutters White ($17)—Australia
King Estate Pinot Gris ($18)—Washington State
Brancott Sauvignon Blanc Reserve ($18)—New Zealand
Bodegas Catena Zapata Chardonnay ($18)—Argentina

RED WINE:

Penfold's Koonunga Hill Shiraz/Cab ($9)—Australia (HW)
Bodegas Castano Hecula ($9)—Spain (HW)
Di Majo Norante Sangiovese ($9)—Italy
Falesco Vitiano IGT ($9)—Italy (HW)
Altos Las Hormigas Malbec ($10)—Argentina
Las Rocas de San Alejandro Garnacha ($10)—Spain
Guigal Cotes du Rhone ($12)—France
Cantele Salice Salentino ($12)—Italy
Bodegas Borsao Tres Picos ($13)—Spain
Abadia Retuerta Rivola ($13)—Spain
Pascal Toso Malbec ($13)—Argentina (HW)
Quinta dos Roques ($14)—Portugal (HW)
Vinas del Cenit Venta Mazzaron ($14)—Spain
Bodegas Castano Solanera ($14)—Spain (HW)
Quinta de Roriz Prazo de Roriz ($15)—Portugal
Chateau Pesquie Cotes du Ventoux Cuvee des Terrasses ($15)
—France
Georges Duboeuf Morgon Jean Descombes ($15)—France
Marquis Philips Shiraz ($16)—Australia (HW)
Falesco Merlot dell'Umbria IGT ($16)—Italy
Mas des Bressades Cabernet/Syrah ($18)—France
Rosenblum Cellars Zinfandel ($18)—California
R Wines Boarding Pass Shiraz ($18)—Australia
Sportoletti Assisi Rosso ($18)—Italy
D'Arenberg The Footbolt Shiraz ($19)—Australia

Bodegas Lan Rioja ($19)—Spain
Allegrini Palazzo della Torre ($19)—Italy
Vietti Barbera d'Asti Tre Vigne ($19)—Italy

DESSERT WINE:

Bonny Doon Muscat Vin de Glaciere ($14)—California (HW)
Quady "Essencia" ($14)—California
Banfi "Rosa Regale" Brachetto d'Acqui ($14)—Italy
La Spinetta Moscato d'Asti Bricco Quaglia ($16)—Italy
Osborne Late Bottled Vintage Porto ($18)—Portugal
Fonseca Bin #27 ($18)—Portugal
Alvear Pedro Ximenez Solera ($19)—Spain

One secret of finding value is to explore wines from regions that are relatively unknown. Although it's possible to find values in Bordeaux and Burgundy and amongst California Cabernets, it takes lots of homework. It's much easier to find bargains from areas that aren't as well known, like Jumilla in Spain, the central Otago of New Zealand, or the Mendoza region in Argentina. And many of the big-name wines from the most well-known regions are truly great and, if the circumstance is right, these wines can also be values.

My parents celebrated their fortieth wedding anniversary in 1990. My dad always spoke of the legendary 1961 Chateau Latour as his favorite of all time. It cost $400, the most I've ever paid for a bottle (it now costs about ten times that amount), but it was a bargain considering the joy we all experienced in sharing it and the lifetime memory it created.

If you want the best value, buy your wine by the case. Most vendors offer a 10 to 20 percent discount for case purchases, but the value goes beyond the lower price. When you have 12 bottles of a fine wine, you can drink one as soon as you bring them home and then enjoy the experience of the wine aging and improving over the years. Buying older, fine wine is a very pricey proposition. Buying newly released fine wine and storing it yourself is the best way to experience exceptional value, not just because the price of the finest wines almost always rises significantly but because of the added pleasure you experience from enjoying the evolution of the wine and knowing that when you're busy at work or doing errands your wine is just laying there getting better every day.

Although the search for value is part of the fun in the enjoyment of wine, it's wise to relax about it and, when in doubt, take the risk of spending more than you may have planned. On your deathbed the pleasure you experienced by sharing fine wine will outweigh your sense of satisfaction at having economized.

Many folks suffer from a fixed notion of the appropriate price to pay for wine. They argue that it's better to spend discretionary income on tangible and more permanent products like jewelry, arts, and crafts. It's true that once the wine is consumed, it's gone, and the empty bottle can't compete with a bracelet or vase. But the pleasure of a fine wine, savored fully at the right time and with the right company, can easily create a lifetime memory. As the playwright Eugene Ionesco (1909-1994) reminds us, *"The ephemeral is the only thing of lasting value."*

10 Great Wine Values from $20-$30

"I think wealth has lost much of its value if it has not wine."
—Ralph Waldo Emerson (1803-1882)
Poet, philosopher, and founder of Transcendentalism

Since the economy tanked, every wine publication offers a regular feature on fine wines under $20. It's relatively easy to find good wines below this price point, and I've shared my favorites with you. But some of the very greatest values require a bit more of an investment. Here are ten recommendations for amazing wines under $30. The higher price of these wines in comparison with the under $20 list buys you a significantly greater level of compexity and potential pleasure. (These are wines that are generally consistent in quality every year. Prices listed are the best I found in the past year).

- **Non-Vintage Champagne from Nicholas Feuillatte, Duval-Leroy, Louis Roederer, Pommery, Heidsieck & Co. Monopole and Piper-Heidsick ($24)**—Non-Vintage champagne represents one of the world's most consistent and magnificent wine values. You can pay $50 or $60 for fine French bubbly, but you can also pay as low as $24 if you shop carefully.

- **Patricia Green Cellars Reserve Pinot Noir ($24)**—Oregon Superb Pinot is hard to find at this price point.

- **Mollydooker Shiraz, The Boxer ($24)**—South Australia Proprietors Sarah and Sparky Marquis live by their motto: "We make wines that make people go wow— through attention to detail and commitment to excellence." This is a great price for so much wow.

- **Bodegas Numanthia, Termes ($25)**—Spain Made from the Tinto del Toro grape (a variation of Tempranillo), this is a lush, opulent, velvety treat.

- **Beringer Knights Valley Cabernet Sauvignon ($25)** —California Fab Cal Cabs under $30 are rarer than steak tartare. Fortunately, Beringer has great distribution, and this wine is easy to find.

- **Columbia Crest Cabernet Sauvignon Reserve ($27)** —Washington State *Wine Spectator* gave the 2005 vintage 95 points! Top names from Washington like Quilceda Creek and Leonetti retail from $85 to well over over $100.

- **Muga Reserva, Rioja ($27)**—Spain Outstanding elegance and complexity.

- **Beringer Private Reserve Chardonnay ($28)**—California All the best qualities of California Chardonnay in one bottle.

The winery lists the price as $35, but this wine is often discounted below $30, and it's flat-out delicious every year.
- **Chateau de Bellevue ($29)**—Lussac, St. Emilion France Organic, excellent, traditionally-styled Bordeaux.
- **Produttori del Barbaresco, Barbaresco ($29)**—Italy The most cost-effective way to experience the charm of the Queen of Wines. Their exceptional single vineyard wines Rabaja´, Paje´, and Asili cost about $60, but they compare favorably with wines from great producers like Giacosa and Gaja whose wines retail well north of $100.

🍇 Score 🍇

Leonardo da Vinci believed that the key to knowledge was "simple and plain experience." He advised his students to avoid "imitating the manner of another" and instead to learn through "first-hand experience, through the five senses."

When it comes to learning about wine, there is no substitute for your own experience and judgment. As you taste and pay attention, you develop greater appreciation and discernment and can make better decisions about what wines to buy. But in a marketplace flooded with rivers of wine from all over the world, how do you decide what to taste?

It helps to know the score. Professional wine critics spend thousands of hours tasting and rating wines. The most influential critic, Robert Parker Jr., paved the way for the overwhelming popularity of the 100-point rating scale. Just like grade school, this scale scores wine from 100 down to 50, A+ to F. This scale has been adopted by many other leading wine reviewers.

Scores offer a convenient shorthand for making a buying assessment. But it's important to find a source for those scores that you can trust. Some retailers offer "in-house" ratings, and many wine publications take advertising revenue from the producers of the wines they rate. This doesn't necessarily disqualify them, but it does suggest that you be wary. The way to find a reliable source for scores is to calibrate your palate with the palate of the critic whose score you rely upon.

In other words, seek recommendations from those whose preferences, tastes, and perspectives suit yours. If you read a recommendation and its accompanying score and then taste the wine you can compare your assessment with the critic's. Over time you will discover how reliable that critic is for you, and in the process you will be developing and refining your own taste. (The same principle applies with your local wine merchant. Tell your local wine merchant the type of wine you like and the amount you are willing to spend and ask for at least three recommendations. Drink, and then assess the value of the recommendations.)

Score Snobs

The economist and poet Kenneth Boulding (1910-1993) said "There are two kinds of people—those who put everything in two groups and those who don't." When it comes to wine scores there are two groups of snobs. Some folks are snobbish about their use of scores—they proclaim: "I don't drink anything under 90 points!" These score snobs are offset by anti-score snobs who look askance at anyone who pays attention to numerical ratings. Among the most egregious of these is the supercilious salesperson who says "It got 92 points from Parker, *if you care about that sort of thing.*"

Robert Parker's popularity can be attributed to his remarkable consistency, unerring gustatory and olfactory memory, uncompromising integrity, and his preference for wines that are purely pleasurable.

Reading wine publications and comparing critical reviews is a great way to learn, but many folks don't have time for this. The scoring system allows wine buyers to make a quick assessment of the likely quality of their purchase. If you discover a highly rated wine from a critic you've learned to trust and you know the price, you can easily quantify the value by considering the points-per-dollar-ratio. If you are hosting a dinner and you've ascertained that your guests want to drink a luscious Australian Shiraz, you can bank on the fact that a score from a critic you trust of, say, 94 points will result in an experience of memorable pleasure for all.

Every issue of Parker's newsletter includes this statement about scores: "Scores are important for the reader to gauge a professional critic's overall qualitative placement of a wine vis-à-vis its peer group. However, it is also vital to consider the description of the wine's style, personality, and potential. No scoring system is perfect, but a system that provides for flexibility in scores, if applied by the same taster without prejudice, can quantify different levels of wine quality and provide the reader with one professional's judgment."

Parker concludes,

"However, there can never be any substitute for your own palate nor any better education than tasting the wine yourself." Amen.

Caveat Emptor: Watch out for the bogus review and the "bait and switch" shelf-talker

Many wine stores place reviews and scores from various critics on the shelf next to the wine. These "shelf talkers" often indicate high scores: 97 POINTS! But always check who gave the rating. Sometimes, the 97 points are bestowed by the merchant, or the winemaker's cousin. If the 97 points are from a legitimate source, then double-check that the wine on the shelf is the same year and type as the one in the review. Also, don't put too much faith in advertisements that trumpet triumphs in regional fairs. The medals awarded at many of these fairs are bit like Little League baseball trophies—everyone gets one just for showing up.

❦ Year (Vintage) ❦

"What cloudless day, what gentle and belated rain
decides that a year, one year among all others,
shall be a great year for wine?
It is a matter in which celestial sorcery is everything."
— Colette (1873-1974), French novelist

How important is the year, or vintage, of your wine? When the great poet Johann Wolfgang Goethe was asked what three treasures he would take with him to the proverbial desert island for a year, he responded: "My collection of poetry books, a beautiful, intelligent woman, and an ample supply of Château Haut-Brion."

He was then asked: "What if you could only bring two? Which of the three would you leave behind?" Goethe didn't hesitate: "The poetry."

The next question, of course, was: "What would you leave behind if only one was allowed?" Goethe reflected for a moment and then responded: "It depends on the vintage."

Vintage matters. Climatic conditions vary from year to year, and despite the alchemical skills of many winemakers the amount and timing of rain and sun has a great effect on each harvest and therefore on the wine in your bottle. Some areas, such as California's Napa Valley or the Barossa region of Australia, tend to enjoy more consistent weather while other regions like France's Cote de Beaune or southern Rhone experience greater variation, but, in any case, it's important to know the relative quality of a given year in order to make a better buying decision.

Let's say, for example, you decide you'd like to try a Chateauneuf du Pape from France's southern Rhone valley, and you happen to see one on a wine list from a good producer, available in both the 2001 and 2002 vintages. Which one will you order? Chances are that the 2002 will be disappointing, as the southern Rhone suffered disastrous floods prior to the harvest that year resulting in a "washed-out" quality in the grapes that survived. (Parker gives the 2002 vintage 59 points out of 100.) And odds are that the 2001, a dry sunny year that led to a relatively small but robust harvest, will be wonderful (96 points from Parker). Of course, you can occasionally find amazing values from off years, and stalwart producers will usually come through even in bad vintages. Moreover, the best producers will sometimes "declassify" their wines in years when the quality is below their high standards. In other words, in such a year a top-of-the-line Brunello di Montalcino won't be offered and instead the wine will be sold as a Rosso di Montalcino at a much lower price. The savvy buyer knows that the off year Rosso is a potentially great value.

And it's difficult to find a Brunello from 1997, 1999, 2001 and 2004, or a Chateauneuf du Pape from 1998, 2001, 2005, and 2007, for example, that *isn't* very good. So, one of the simplest, easiest guides to choosing fine wine is to make a note of the best years for your preferred types of wine and slip it in your wallet or purse, or leave yourself a memo on your Blackberry or iPhone. You can consult Parker's vintage rating chart— it is available free on his website —and there's a vintage chart included in most issues of *Wine Spectator* magazine.

TIPPSY is an easy way to remember how to make wine-buying decisions. Consider the Types of wine you like. Check the available Inventory of the wines you seek. Learn the names of some of the best Producers. Consider the Price and check comparables in your search for the incomparable. Knowing the Score from a critic you trust can save time, but always be true to your own palate. And, learn the best Years of the wines you like.

The WINO Principles: Matching Food and Wine

"The flavor of a food almost always reveals the quality of a wine and exalts it. In turn, the quality of a wine complements the pleasure of a food and spiritualizes it."
—Luigi Veronelli (1926-2004),
Italian culinary philosopher

One of the great things about being a grown-up is that you can eat and drink whatever you want. In pairing food and wine at home, you can be true to your own taste and have whatever you like with whatever you like whenever you like it.

When you are ordering wine for others, however, it's important to have some guidelines for matching food and wine. Although your first concern as a host is always to match the wine to the people and the circumstances, it also helps to have a basic understanding of wine and food compatibility.

Most people know that white wine is generally better with seafood and red with meat, but there are plenty of exceptions to this standard. (For example, try grilled Oregon king salmon with wild mushrooms and a Pinot Noir from Domaine Serene, Ken Wright or Cristom; or enjoy a platter of charcuterie with an Alsatian Riesling from Hugel et Fils, Zind-Humbrecht or Domaine Weinbach.)

When it comes to pairing wine and food there are four considerations that are at least as important as the color of the wine. WINO is a simple acronym for helping you remember these:

Weight: Common sense suggests that you match a heavier dish with a heavier wine, a lighter dish with a lighter wine. A New Zealand Pinot Noir isn't likely to be hefty enough to stand up to an osso bucco and a Barossa Valley Shiraz will probably crush a lighter veal dish.

Intensity: Align the intensity of flavors in the food with the intensity of the wine. Spicy pasta puttanesca calls for a wine with bold flavors, like a rich Nero d'Avola from southern Italy, while a simple poached white fish calls for a less intense wine.

If your food and wine are on different wavelengths of weight or intensity you can still create a happy marriage as long as you follow the counsel of the legendary Master of Wine Michael Broadbent, who advises: "Decide which is the soloist and which is the accompanist."

No-nos:

A few combinations to avoid:

• Chewing gum, breath mints, Pez, mouthwash, and toothpaste don't pair well with any wine.

• Strong cocktails will obliterate your sensitivity to the nuances of food-wine pairing. The grandmaster of all 3-star chefs, Fernand Point (1897-1955), warned, "After one cocktail, or worse yet, two, the palate can no more distinguish a bottle of Mouton Rothschild from a bottle of ink!"

• Dry wine with sweet food tends to taste like battery acid. As a friend recently wrote: "Last night I experienced the unfortunate combination of Oreo cookies and Sauvignon Blanc. Yuk! I've learned from my mistake."

• Very hot chilies with any complex, subtle wine will result in the loss of the subtlety and complexity.

• Strong vinegars and highly acidic foods can obscure the nuances of flavor in many fine wines.

• Be wary of artichokes, asparagus, mint, and eggs. Artichokes contain a chemical called cynarin that, for some people, distorts the flavor of wine. Asparagus contains methyl mercaptan, which can make fine wine taste like vegetable juice. Mint is a no-no because it dominates your sense of smell and you then have no nose

for the wine (undertakers traditionally kept a sprig of mint available to assuage the unpleasant aromas associated with their craft). And egg yolks tend to function as wine flavor prophylactics, coating the palate and interfering with full enjoyment.
• Most importantly, please don't worry about getting pairings right or wrong. Take an exploratory approach and have fun discovering what works for you and your guests.

If you are out to dinner and one of your guests orders an omelet stuffed with artichokes and asparagus, seasoned with mint, vinegar, and jalapeno peppers just relax and make the most of the experience. People's feelings are always more important than the correctness of the pairing. When you're faced with food and wine that don't go together you can use a bite of bread and butter to clear the less than harmonious flavors from your palate before you sip your wine.

> *"The perfect marriage of food and wine
> should allow room for infidelity."*
> —Roy Andries de Groot (1910-1983),
> *In Search of the Perfect Meal*

Origin: Origin offers a wonderful clue to some of the world's greatest food and wine pairings. In many cases, all you need to know is, "If it grows together, it goes together." Fernand Point of the legendary La Pyramide restaurant near Lyon in southern France had a wine cellar filled with the greatest treasures of Burgundy and Bordeaux. But, when asked, Point always preferred to recommend the wines from nearby Cote Rotie and Condrieu to accompany the local ingredients that were featured in his incomparable cuisine.
Classic wine and food combinations that originate in the same geographical and cultural milieu include those from:

- **Provence, southern France:** Saffron-scented fresh fish stew (*bouillabaisse*) and Rosé wines like those from Domaine Ott and Domaine Tempier.
- **Chavignol, Loire Valley, France:** Goat's milk cheese (*crottin de chavignol*) is a perfect match with a white Sancerre from Francois Cotat, Gerard Boulay, or Henri Bourgeois.
- **Priorato in Catalonia, Spain:** Goose or duck with turnips *(oca, amp naps)* and regional red wines such as Clos Mogador, Cellers Pasanau, and Vall Llach.
- **Tuscany, Italy:** Broad noodles with wild boar sauce (*pappardelle al ragu di cinghiale*) and a Chianti Classico from Fattoria di Felsina, Fontodi, or Castello di Monsanto; Florentine Chianina beefsteak (*bistecca alla fiorentina*) and Brunello di Montalcino from Fuligni, Uccelliera, or Il Poggione.

These regional marriages of food and wine are the expression of centuries of practical wisdom. The soil and microclimate that nurtures the foliage upon which native cows, goats, geese, ducks, and pigs feed is the same as that which gives life to the vines. The flavor essences that emerge all spring from the same nutrient and ambient source, creating legendary harmony.

As a TIPPSY WINO you will remember how to buy wine and match it with food. And sometimes it's best, when you have a truly exceptional wine, to find a perfect setting with someone you love and focus purely on the wine without any food. On the other hand, it's fair to say that great wine goes with almost everything. If the wine is good enough, and you avoid the no-nos, then everyone will almost always be happy with it.

Shabby-Chic Wine and Food

What's the right wine to accompany take-out Chinese food? How about Mexican, Indian or Thai? Natalie MacLean is devoted to helping you find something wonderful to drink with anything you eat, even Jell-O! She enthuses, "You really can drink wine with just about anything." She adds, "With modern fusion cuisine and wines from new regions around the world, the choices—and confusion—are great."

Here are 10 fun, "shabby-chic" food and wine matches:
1. Macaroni and cheese with Chardonnay
2. Nachos with Zinfandel
3. Popcorn with Champagne
4. Pizza with Barbera or Chianti
5. Chinese food with Riesling
6. Cheeseburgers with Shiraz
7. Turkey burgers with Pinot Noir
8. Quiche with Sauvignon Blanc
9. Curry with Gewürztraminer
10. Meatloaf with Cabernet Sauvignon

The 7 Wine and Food Pairings You Must Experience Before You Die

> *"When what you're drinking melds with what you're eating, something magical takes place."*
> —Karen Page and Andrew Dornenburg,
> *What to Drink with What You Eat*

What are the most magical food and wine pairings? This question is the inspiration for a lifelong exploration. There are always new discoveries and unexpected delights awaiting us on the hedonic path. One way to recognize a great pairing is that each bite of food makes you yearn for another sip of the wine, and each sip of wine makes you lust for another bite of the food. And great pairings are unforgettable: the tastes, aromas, textures, the overall experience—it becomes a lifetime memory of pleasure.

If you have the opportunity to see some the wonders of the world like the Parthenon in Athens, the pyramids in Egypt or Michelangelo's David in Florence, chances are that you will be astounded by their magnificence. The wine and food pairings presented here are all astoundingly delicious, and if you haven't tried them yet you will wonder why you waited so long. Of course, there are many other wonderful combinations. This list isn't intended to be definitive, but everyone I know who has tried these pairings has been transported to a realm of speechless, endorphin-marinated bliss. All of these pairings are relatively easy to experience. There are no complex recipes, but some of the ingredients can be pricey, although for lifetime memories they all represent great value. The web links provided are the ones used for ordering these delicacies online when they weren't available in local markets. There are two wine recommendations listed for each pairing. The first wine listed is the ideal choice from among the many wines tasted, the second wine listed is the most extraordinary value. The vintages mentioned are the ones that were enjoyed in the extensive research behind this chapter. If you can't find these, then seek the best available vintage.

FRESH PASTA WITH WHITE TRUFFLES AND BARBARESCO

"I have simple tastes— the very best satisfies me every time."
— Oscar Wilde (1854-1900), Irish poet and playwright

My dear friends Karen Page and Andrew Dornenburg are two-time James Beard award-winning food and wine writers. They dine out regularly, often at the chef's table of the finest restaurants in the world. A couple of years ago I called them up on my way to New York (in late October, truffle season) and, knowing that Andrew is a world-class chef, I made the following offer: "You cook something with white truffles, and I will bring the vino." Well, Andrew rose to the occasion. He met his truffle connection downtown (cash only) and scored two gorgeous fungi. For our first course he prepared a perfect fresh pasta with, as Karen described it on the delightful menu she printed up for our dinner, "Lots of freshly shaved white truffle." The wine for that course was the 2000 Bruno Giacosa Santo Stefano Barbaresco. How good was it? Well, when we get together for food and wine there's usually plenty of playful, imaginative, and nuanced language flying around, but in this case we were all speechless at the pure perfection of the combination. Then I witnessed a tear of joy fall slowly from Karen's right eye. What is the magic that can evoke that depth of reaction from one of the most sophisticated palates on the planet?

White truffles, aka *Tuber magnatum,* are one of the most prized delicacies in the culinary universe. At a recent auction a magnate from Hong Kong paid $210,000 for a 750-gram tuber from Alba in Italy. That's a pricey fungus. But, when they are right, white truffles justify your investment. The great composer Rossini referred to them as "The Mozart of mushrooms."

Truffle hunters use trained dogs to sniff these "white diamonds" out of the Langhe, Italy, earth. Truffles look like lumpy, small potatoes. A good one will be weighty, compact, and firm. But the real test is when you slice it and inhale.

If you go to a fine Italian restaurant from mid-October until about New Year's Eve you will know that they are on the menu when the door opens, because you'll be greeted with a distinctively seductive aroma. Truffles are renowned as an aphrodisiac, but that's probably just because they smell like good sex. As poet and naturalist Diane Ackerman explains in *The Natural History of the Senses,* the scent of truffles "make one's loins smolder like those of randy lions."

And you won't have to pay six-figures for the pleasure. Prices for a few shavings on your risotto or pasta vary dramatically, from around $30 to upwards of $100. If you're flush, you can order some for yourself; if not, just sit near someone who has ordered them and inhale. For the very best experience, buy your own personal white truffle.

The Piemontese like something called Fonduta made from cheese, eggs, milk and truffles, and some folks prefer risotto or scrambled eggs as the base, but for the supreme food and wine pairing nothing beats a bowl of fresh pasta, perhaps a taglioni or fettucine, with butter, parmesan cheese, and lots of freshly shaved white truffle. A classic example of the O in WINO, the perfect pairing with this dish is a fine Barbaresco, the queen of wines, originating in the same Piemonte soil that yields the truffle. Bruno Giacosa "Santo Stefano" (1985, 2000), Giusseppe Cortese "Rabaja" (2001)

Truffle Tips

Don't wash your truffle until you are ready to enjoy it. "The dirt keeps in the aroma," according to Italian food authority Marcella Hazan. She recommends wrapping your fabulous fungus in paper towels and then aluminum foil, before refrigerating. When truffles are sold at deli counters you will often see them displayed in a jar with rice, but this isn't the optimal way to store them, unless you want to make a risotto with that rice. If you're on a tight budget then you can substitute white truffle-infused olive oil, or truffle salt, for a similar heavenly effect. Everything you might ever want to know about truffles you can learn by reading: *Taming The Truffle: the History, Lore, and Science of the Ultimate Mushroom* by Ian Hall, Gordon Brown, and Alessandra Zambonelli. You can order truffles via the internet at: www.trufflemarket.com

CHABLIS AND OYSTERS

What's the most seductive food in the world? The legendary Venetian lover Giacomo Casanova (1725-1798) believed that there was nothing more conducive to amorous activity than sharing some quivering, plump, juicy oysters.

If your lover isn't around to share them, then the next best combination for a plate of fresh oysters is a crisp white wine. Simple and perfect. Hemingway describes it in *A Moveable Feast*, "As I ate the oysters with their strong taste of the sea and their faint metallic taste that the cold white wine washed away, leaving only the sea taste and the succulent texture, and as I drank their liquid from each shell and washed it down with the crisp taste of the wine, I lost the empty feeling and began to be happy and make plans."

Planning the perfect match with oysters will make you happy because there are many lovely options. An informal poll of my oyster and wine-loving friends yielded nominees including Sancerre, dry Spanish Sherry, Pinot Grigio, Muscadet, dry Alsatian Rieslings, Champagne, Sauternes, and Guinness Stout. Which one is the most sublime?

Palates differ and so do oysters. There are many varieties, but the best offer a unique combination of sumptuous, erotic texture and minerally, briny, and sometimes slightly sweet taste. Satirist and poet, Jonathan Swift (1667-1745), remarked, "It was a bold man who first ate an oyster," but after the first one, it's hard to stop. You can fine-tune this marvelous pairing by experimenting with specific wines for each oyster variety, attempting to discover the ultimate match for Kumamotos, Olympias, or Belons, but there is one wine that reigns supreme as the perfect marriage for them all: Chablis. Why Chablis? Most other crisp whites act as refreshing palate cleansers, and they can be memorable in combination with oysters, but fine Chablis will also clear the gustatory deck while offering a seductive, haunting complexity of oyster-shell, limestone, and fresh peach aromas and flavors ranging from ripe pears and sea salt to caramelized lemon and beyond. And the grapes for Chablis are grown in the Burgundy region of France where the soil is largely composed of ancient, fossilized oyster shells.

Domaine Francois Raveneau Chablis les Clos (2002), Domaine Vocoret Chablis Premier Cru Montmains (2004).

Oysterology

Read: *A Geography of Oysters: The Connoisseur's Guide to Oyster Eating in North America* by Rowan Jacobsen. Washington State's Taylor Shellfish Farms sponsors an annual Pacific Coast Oyster Wine Competition. www.oysterwine.com. You can have fresh oysters delivered overnight from the world-famous Pike Place Fish Market (www.pikeplacefish.com).

CHAMPAGNE, PARMESAN CHEESE, AND MARCONA ALMONDS

"Champagne is more than a drink, it is also a state of mind."
— Rosemary Zraly, aka-*The Champagne Lady*

If I had to choose just one type of wine to drink every night it would be Champagne. Fortunately, I don't have to choose, so I will celebrate that freedom by opening a bottle of Champagne.

Champagne is great with almost everything, and it's perfect by itself. Purists question the classic matches with caviar or smoked salmon, but don't refuse these if someone offers. Champagne is super with sushi and, believe it or not, Remy Krug of the Krug Champagne family recommends popcorn as the ideal foil for his estate's legendary multi-vintage bubbly.

When it comes to bringing out the best qualities of fine Champagne, the combination of chunks of aged parmesan cheese from Parma, Mantua, Modena, or Bologna, Italy, and Marcona almonds from Andalucia, Spain, is unbeatable.

Marcona almonds, fried in olive oil and salted, should come with a warning label because their creamy-crunchy-lush texture and rich, salty taste make them addictive.

Enjoy a few almonds and then a sip of Champagne. Then let a small chunk of aged Parmigiano-Reggiano melt in your mouth. The aging process results in a flavor- concentrating granular texture. Have another sip of Champagne...and you'll want the next almond...Champagne...cheese...Champagne...almond...Bliss!

You can add another level of refinement and pleasure by warming your Marcona almonds in the oven for a minute or two, then place them in three small bowls and dust each bowl with a different type of artisan salt. Try, for example, the Murray River Flake Salt, Fleur De Sel de Guérande, and Alaea Hawaiian Sea Salt (www.artisansalt.com).

Duval-Leroy "Femme" (1995), 'Cuvee Reserve', Pierre Peters.

THE ULTIMATE HAM AND CHEESE: IBERICO BELLOTA HAM AND MANCHEGO CHEESE WITH TEMPRANILLO.

Ham doesn't usually qualify as health food, but the Iberico is a delicious exception. (The meat contains 55 percent oleic acid. Only extra-virgin olive oil has a higher natural percentage of this healthy mono-unsaturated fatty acid.) These free-range porkers dine on herbs, grasses, and acorns (*bellota* is Spanish for acorn). It's best to enjoy gossamer-thin slices on a warm platter, so that the fat begins to melt. As you place a slice on your tongue the ham seems to evaporate in a nutty, rich, savory haze. You can taste the essence of the Spanish forest pasture. Just as a great wine reveals many of its best qualities after you swallow it, the "finish" of the finest Iberico ham is a revelation.

A crusty fresh bread and a few chunks of aged Manchego and/or Iberico cheese set the stage for an exquisite Tempranillo from Ribera del Duero, Toro, or Rioja.

Vega Sicilia Unico Reserva (1970), Muga Reserva (2004)

(You can order Iberico Bellota and fine aged Manchego from www.tienda.com)

JACK STACK'S CROWN PRIME RIB OF BEEF AND A MASSIVE AUSSIE SHIRAZ

Novelist and wine writer Jay McInerney poses the eternal question for lovers of the greatest antipodean reds: "What to eat with a massive Aussie Shiraz." He suggests, "grilled Tyrannosaurus Rex steaks rubbed with chili."

The next best thing to dining on dinosaur is to be found in Kansas City.

In my travels around the United States, I'm always seeking the best BBQ. North Carolina, Tennessee and Texas are all high on my smoked meat radar. A few years ago I was leading a seminar in Kansas City. My hotel was non-descript and so was the hotel restaurant. I went to the front desk and asked the nice ladies on duty; "Hey, this is Kansas

City. There must be some good steak or BBQ in the area?" They both smiled and then said in unison, " The top-rated BBQ restaurant in the country is one mile from here!"

They arranged for the hotel van to drive me down the road to the legendary Jack Stack BBQ. After a twenty-minute wait I was seated at my own booth, where I experienced one of the great things about America: A young waiter, who had recently come to Kansas City from Mumbai, India, asked me what I would like. I asked him, " What's the absolute best thing on the menu?"

Without hesitation he responded, "Oh sir, you must try the Crown Prime Ribs of Beef."

When you order the Crown Prime Ribs of Beef for the first time, you will be taken aback when the platter arrives. The three huge beef ribs seem like more than anyone could eat, except perhaps Fred Flinstone. But after your first smoky, umami-rich bite, time will disappear and so will the meat. The good news is that Jack Stack will deliver these to your door. While you're heating the ribs, open a bottle—actually a magnum might be more appropriate—of the most mouth staining, monster Shiraz you can find. Although some of the other food and wine wonders described in this chapter offer more subtle pleasures, this combination is sheer, unabashed hedonism. (For the perfect wine and food pairing, skip the sauce and use just a little of the dry rub.)

Clarendon Hills Astralis (1996), R Wines Boarding Pass Shiraz First Class (2005). (www.jackstackbbq.com)

VINTAGE PORT WITH REAL BLUE STILTON CHEESE AND WALNUTS

Evelyn Waugh (1903 -1966), author of *Brideshead Revisited*, described port as "the comfort of age and the companion of the scholar and the philosopher." You don't have to be old or scholarly to enjoy one of the world's truly great wines. As for philosophy, Louis Pasteur noted, "A bottle of wine contains more philosophy than all the books in the world." And a bottle of vintage port may be the most highly extracted form of liquid philosophy. Best enjoyed at the end of a perfect meal with colleagues and friends, port is especially conducive to philosophical musing and social bonding.

In traditional British custom, the host fills the glass of the guest sitting to his right and then passes the decanter to the left (the "port" side in British Naval parlance). That guest fills the host's glass and passes the port along in a clockwise rotation until the decanter returns to the host. If the progress of the port is stalled, one doesn't ask for the decanter directly. Instead, the person who has delayed the bottle's progression is asked, "I say, do you know the Bishop of Norwich?" This is a reference to a blathering bishop known for descanting endlessly while remaining oblivious to those awaiting their port. Those in the know will immediately pass the port, but ignorance of the ritual may result in a response such as "Can't say that I do." And the traditional reply is "He's a jolly nice fellow, but he never seems to remember to *pass the port*."

Another aspect of traditional port etiquette is that the entire bottle is enjoyed before the evening is out. This usually isn't an issue since fine vintage port is so good that guests often feel it's the simply the best wine they've ever tasted.

The ideal accompaniment is the "king of cheeses," Stilton. British author G. K. Chesterton (1874-1936) was a gourmand who tipped the scales at almost three hundred pounds. He once commented to his much slimmer friend, the playwright, wine-lover, and notorious wit George Bernard Shaw, "To look at you, one would think that England was struck by famine." Shaw shot back, "To look at you, one would think you caused it." Many great poets have been inspired by wine, but Chesterton is one of the few to offer an ode to cheese. He observed, "Poets have been mysteriously silent on the subject of cheese." Chesterton filled this poetic lacuna with his "Sonnet to a Stilton Cheese." It begins:

> *"Stilton, thou shouldst be living at this hour*
> *And so thou art. Nor losest grace thereby;*
> *England has need of thee, and so have I."*

Stilton doesn't actually come from the village of Stilton after which it is named. Real Stilton is made in just three counties: Derbyshire, Leicestershire, Nottinghamshire, and there are only seven dairies licensed to make it. Among these, the most highly recommended is Colston Bassett Stilton from Nottinghamshire.

Stilton is a magical juxtaposition of creamy, silky texture and lush, piquant flavors. The magic is amplified when you enjoy a nibble of Stilton followed by a freshly cracked walnut and then a sip of vintage port.

Taylor Fladgate (1963), Fonseca (1994).

THE STUFF OF DREAMS

You can add to the enjoyment of the Port and Stilton ritual by including classic accoutrements such as the Hoggett Decanter and the Stilton Spoon. The Hoggett Decanter preempts Norwichian tendencies to hog the port. Its rounded bottom makes it impossible to set it down on the table until it is returned to its station next to the host—a specially crafted wooden base into which it nestles snugly. And there's no better way to enjoy your Stilton than to scoop it right out of the center of a full cylinder with a long silver spoon.

Of course, you can skip all the rituals or make up your own, but this combination is the stuff upon which dreams are made. Indeed, the British Cheese Board conducted a study in 2005 showing that more than 75 percent of those who enjoyed a modest serving of Stilton before bedtime had unusually vivid dreams.

Our pale day is sinking into twilight,
And if we sip the wine, we find dreams coming upon us
Out of the imminent night.
— D. H. Lawrence (1885-1930),
English author, poet, and playwright

CHATEAU D'YQUEM AND???

There are many great wines in the world. But as a wine-lover there's only one that you absolutely must try before you die: Chateau d'Yquem. Praised by Thomas Jefferson and George Washington, d'Yquem was also the favorite wine of Alexandre Dumas, Honoré de Balzac, Marcel Proust, and Jules Verne (and Hannibal Lecter).

Y'quem's unique, uncanny harmony of yin and yang qualities makes it surprisingly compatible with a wide range of foods, most notably oysters, Roquefort cheese, foie gras, or pear tart tatin.

Whatever you have with it, the wine is the soloist and the dish will be the accompanist. It probably goes best with kissing. If you are having it for the first time, drink it on a sunny afternoon with your sweetheart. Then finish the bottle later that night, after dinner.

As Robert Parker writes in his classic *Bordeaux*, "There is no other wine in the world like it, and there is no other luxury wine that can possibly justify its price as much as Yquem. The remarkable amount of painstaking labor necessary to produce the nectar known as Yquem is almost impossible to comprehend."

Although it's expensive, the good news is that a half-bottle is plenty for two people. Look for the following vintages to drink now: 1983, 1986, 1988, 1989, 1990, and 1997. For your future happiness consider laying down the 2001, 2003, 2005, and 2007.

AND ANOTHER SUPREME PLEASURE...

We can't leave the subject of the greatest wine and food pairings without discussing one of life's supreme pleasures: chocolate. First cultivated by the Maya, the cacao bean actually became a form of currency in the Aztec empire. According to the Aztecs, cocoa consumption inspired courage, wisdom, and enlightenment. Introduced to Europe by the Spanish conquistadors in the early sixteenth century, chocolate was a treat reserved for royals and nobles until mass production methods were developed in the nineteenth century (hallelujah!).

Chocolate makes you smarter!

At a recent annual meeting of the American Association for the Advancement of Science, Professor Ian MacDonald of the University of Nottingham presented a paper supporting the conclusion that eating dark chocolate can raise alertness and temporarily improve performance in a range of cognitive tasks. MacDonald's report is one of an increasing number of scientific studies demonstrating the benefits of moderate consumption of high-quality dark chocolate. Reporting on a broad survey of research in *Health* magazine, Frances Largeman-Roth concludes that dark chocolate "can lower blood pressure, improve skin, and give us a thrill that rivals a passionate kiss." The ingredients responsible for these benefits are known as "flavanols," also found in green tea, blueberries, and red wine.

The legendary epicure Brillat-Savarin noted "It has been shown as proof positive that carefully prepared chocolate is as healthful a food as it is pleasant; that it is nourishing and easily digested. . . that it is above all helpful to people who must do a great deal of mental work."

When it comes to choosing your chocolate, seek out the pure and unadulterated —avoid chocolates with emulsifiers, lecithin and other vegetable fats or flavorings. For an easily available high-quality treat buy a bar each of the artisan chocolates from Scharffen Berger (62%, 70%, and 82% cacao content) and/or Theo (look for their Origin signature line -74%, 75% and 84% cacao) and enjoy a wonderful comparative tasting. Chocolatiers usually recommend that you taste in ascending order of cocoa percentage.

As you explore the cacao percentage that you prefer, you can begin comparing chocolates from different producers with the same cacao percentage. Artisan chocolatier and founder of NOKA Chocolates (www.nokachocolate.com) Katrina Merrem explains, "When you compare fine chocolates that are, for example, 75 percent cacao, this means that the sugar content is the same (25 percent), so the difference in perceptions of aroma, sweetness, flavor and mouth-feel are attributable solely to the nuances of the particular beans and not the varying amounts of sugar."

Although you don't get to swirl or spit your chocolate, the process of enjoying it has many parallels to wine tasting. Take a moment to appreciate the color and glossiness of your bar. Break off a bite-size piece and listen for what chocolate adepts call "the snap." The best chocolate makes a crisp sound when you break it. Breathe in the aromas, and then place a small piece in your mouth and let it slowly dissolve on your tongue. You can release bursts of flavor by sucking and chewing very gently, but this is optional because high-quality chocolate will melt in your mouth. (Cocoa butter melts at 97°F, just below normal body temperature of 98.6°F.)

Just like wine, savor the aromas, mouth-feel, and flavors. (Aromas and flavors may range from fruity—cherry, banana, raisin—to spicy—cinnamon, vanilla, cardamom—to flowery—lavender, rose, hibiscus—and beyond.) Take a few moments to savor the aftertaste before you sip your wine. Like fine wine, great chocolate expresses the unique properties of the soil and microclimate where it was cultivated. For advanced appreciation you can try chocolate from single origin beans from different producers, or you can create a theme around a country (Madagascar, Ghana, Indonesia, Venezuela) or a type of bean (there are three main varieties of cacao: forastero, criollo, and trinitario—the later two are preferred by the cognoscenti).

The main thing to remember about pairing wine and chocolate is that unlike the other delights we've explored in which the wine is the soloist or an equal partner with the food, in this case the food is the soloist. For your soloist to shine, you want to pair her with a wine that is at least as sweet as she is. When the chocolate is sweeter than the wine each sip seems sour. And because even the darkest chocolate coats your tongue, it's a good idea to enjoy it with a wine that also offers enough acidity to refresh your palate.

For optimum enjoyment serve the chocolates with as many of the following wines as you can find and ask your guests to decide which pairing they like best. These recommendations are the top choices from a number of memorable trials:

- **Domaine du Mas Blanc (Dr. Parce) Banyuls Rimage Cuvee la Coume-Banyuls** is a Grenache-based wine from the Languedoc-Roussillon area of France. Dr. Parce is among the greatest producers.
- **Mas Amiel Maury Vintage Privilege**—Another scrumptious treat from the Languedoc-Roussillon area.
- **Philip Togni Ca Togni**—This is a magical red Muscat dessert wine made by one of California's great masters of Cabernet Sauvignon.
- **Rosemount "Old Benson" Fine Old Tawny Port**—In addition to the chocolate, try this Australian "sticky" with walnuts and organic Turkish apricots.
- **Barolo Chinato**—This is a specialty after-dinner drink from Italy's Piedmonte region made with aged Barolo wine and a combination of botanicals, including the bark of the local cinchona tree. Developed by the legendary winemaker and pharmacist Giuseppe Cappellano in the 1870s, it is renowned as an aid to digestion and is the single greatest pairing with fine chocolate I've yet to discover. The best Barolo Chinato producers include Cerretto and Cappellano.

Almond Joys, Orange Passions, Raspberry Pleasures

If you like almonds with your chocolate then you will adore the nutty flavor of a great Spanish sherry. Look for these phenomenal values: 1927 Alvear Pedro Ximenez Solera or the Alvear Solera Cream sherry.

If you prefer chocolate-covered orange slices or orange peel, you must try Quady Essencia, a plush Orange Muscat dessert wine from California.

If you insist on raspberries with your chocolate then go for California's Bonny Doon Vineyard Framboise.

Food and Wine and Sex: The Poetry of the Senses

When I cook for friends they sometimes ask if I'd consider opening a restaurant. Although I admire professional chefs and restaurateurs it's not something to which I aspire. I love food and wine and wouldn't want to exchange them for money. Asking someone if they'd cook for money seems a bit like asking your lover, "Have you ever thought of doing this professionally?"

Food and sex do, however, go hand-in-hand. Perhaps you noticed that the descriptions of truffles, oysters, d'Yquem, and chocolate all involved erotic references?

Which is better, food or sex? This is a topic for lively discussion, but it seems clear that food is the more reliable pleasure. Your thinly sliced Iberico ham doesn't have to be in the mood to be eaten. You can have it whenever you want (although it is better if you let it melt on a warm plate before devouring it). When you eat Italian food, Indian cuisine doesn't get jealous. And food can be enjoyed three times a day, every day. Of course, the ideal scenario involves a combination of these delights.

In a classic *Seinfeld* episode, George Costanza aims to combine his three favorite activities by having sex while eating a pastrami sandwich and watching television. As George's date informs him, however, these activities are best enjoyed sequentially rather than simultaneously.

It's not uncommon for gourmands to express their pleasure in dining with erotic allusions. Delicious dishes are often described as "like sex," "erotic," and "orgasmic." But although an attractive person is considered a "dish," the use of food descriptors probably isn't the best way to compliment your lover. Nevertheless, sharing food and wine with a partner, or prospective partner, is one of the most reliable catalysts for romance. The more delicious and sensually enlivening the food and wine experience, the greater the desire to follow the experience with love-making. And what better way to work up an appetite than to make love?

If you are single and assessing a prospective partner, dining is one of the best ways to learn about your date's attitude to the sensual world. The way someone eats and drinks offers plenty of clues to behavior in the bedroom. If you are part of a couple, then sharing special meals and fine wines together is one of the best ways to keep the magic alive in your relationship. As the great gourmand Honoré de Balzac (1799-1850), author of *The Elixir of Life* reminds us, "Love is the poetry of the senses."

PART 2

THE ELIXIR OF GENIUS

The Lifeblood
of Civilization

*"Wine advanced the progress of civilization.
It facilitated the contacts between distant
cultures, providing the motive and the means of
trade, bringing strangers together in high
spirits and with open minds."*
—Hugh Johnson

Wine is the lifeblood of civilization, the symbol of spiritual blessing and the elixir of genius. When you open a bottle of wine and share it with your friends or colleagues, you are expressing your connection with an ancient, vivifying cultural practice. You are linking with a tradition that has inspired many of the greatest minds in human history.

Although scientists have discovered fossilized vines estimated to be sixty million years old, the earliest evidence of wine was found in a jar discovered in Persia, dating from the year 5400 B.C. Hieroglyphs on tombs from 2600 B.C. show that the ancient Egyptians cultivated vineyards. Wine was the preferred drink at the courts of the pharaohs and a favored offering to the gods. A team of Spanish researchers recently confirmed that King Tutankhamen was a red wine drinker, and we know, from the inscriptions on the many statues that portray him holding cups of wine, that Amenhotep the 3rd (eighteenth dynasty) attributed his exceptional strength and athletic prowess to wine. Wine was also an essential accompaniment in Egyptian funerary rites and no noble would consider being entombed without it.

Humanity's oldest epic poem, the Babylonian *Gilgamesh*, dates back more than four thousand years. Seeking eternal life, the hero discovers its secret in "the realm of the sun," where he finds an enchanted vineyard, described thus:

It bears rubies for fruit,
Hung with grape clusters, lovely to look on
Lapis lazuli are its branches,
It bears fruit, desirable to see.

The Gilgamesh epic features a heroic quest, a flood, an ark filled with animals, and wine. The story of Noah, the Bible's first vintner, recapitulates these elements and is one of the more than 250 references to wine throughout the text. Although the Bible contains many cautions against overindulgence, wine is predominantly portrayed as a divine gift. In the Book of Judges we learn that "Wine ... cheereth God and man." The Book of Psalms hails, "Wine that maketh glad the heart of man. " In Ecclesiastes we are advised, "Go, therefore, eat your bread with joy and drink your wine with cheer." Jesus shared wine with his disciples to celebrate Passover (Manischewitz?) in what became known as "The Last Supper." Christ's first miracle involved the transformation of water into wine at a wedding, and he referred to himself as "the True Vine." The importance of wine in both Hebrew and Christian ritual can't be overstated.

Two thousand years before the time of Christ, Chinese civilization was already well advanced, and as Hugh Johnson points out, "wine was an important part of it." Johnson quotes the director of Taiwan's National Palace Museum, who explains that drinking wine was a "favored pastime of heroic figures and poets since ancient times, and has contributed to the creation of countless masterpieces in the history of human culture."

Three Great Confluences of Wine and Genius

*"To take wine into your mouth
is to savor a droplet of the river of human history."*
—Clifton Fadiman (1904-1999),
author, editor, and television personality

A full consideration of the role of wine in the creation of masterpieces throughout human culture would result in a vast encyclopedia. In this chapter we will sip some of the highlights. There are three great confluences of genius that propelled the Western world to its greatest achievements: The ancient Greeks, the Renaissance, and the founding fathers of the United States of America. The love of wine is one thing that each of these extraordinary flowerings of genius has in common.

The Ancient Greeks: The Original Toga Party

"The peoples of the Mediterranean began to emerge from barbarism when they learnt to cultivate the olive and the vine."
—Thucydides (Fifth century, B.C.), Greek historian

A few years ago I had the opportunity to visit the ancient Athenian Agora. I was thrilled to walk in the footsteps of Socrates, Plato, and the other geniuses who launched our civilization. The Agora was the original Athenian city center and shopping mall, and the birthplace of the first democracy. Citizens assembled there to conduct business, talk politics, adjudicate legal matters, share stories and poems, drink wine, and speculate on the essential nature of creation.

The original Greek philosophers, known as the pre-Socratics, all theorized about the fundamental composition of the universe. Thales (c.624 BC–c.546 BC) proposed a world composed of water, while Anaximenes (c. 585 BC–c. 525 BC) championed the notion that air was the essential ingredient of creation. Pythagoras (c. 572 BC–c.490 BC) propounded the idea that the universe was composed of numbers and music, and Democritus (c. 460 BCE–c. 370 BCE) put forward the theory that everything was made of atoms. Judging by their customs and practice, however, it seems that the ancient Greek world was really made of wine.

Without the Greeks and their love of wine and poetry we would-n't have our culture, and we might not even have our language. In *Guns, Germs, and Steel,* Jared Diamond writes, "Greek alphabetic writing from the moment of its appearance was a vehicle of poetry and humor, to be read in private homes." Diamond explains that the first preserved example of Greek alphabetic writing is a line of poetry inscribed on an Athenian wine jug of about 740 B.C. He adds, "The earliest preserved examples of the Etruscan and Roman alphabets are also inscriptions on drinking cups and wine containers."

The poetry on the wine jug that Diamond describes dates back to the time of Homer, the seminal Greek poet. No one knows for certain the date of the Homer's birth or death but scholars guess that he lived between 800-700 BC. His *Iliad* and *Odyssey* are universally acclaimed as seminal works of Western Culture. Homer's description of "the wine-dark sea" and his contention that, "The weary find new strength in generous wine" are examples of the constant stream of oenological references in his works. Homer pays tribute to the power of wine but also cautions about the *veritas* in vino: "The wine urges me on, the be-witching wine, which sets even a wise man to singing and to laughing gently and rouses him up to dance and brings forth words which were better unspoken." He adds, "Wine is a magician for it loosens the tongue and liberates good stories."

Homer brings the gods of ancient Greece to life, including, of course, the god of wine. The son of Zeus and the mortal woman Semele, Dionysus, later known by the Romans as Bacchus, was the

Greek god of wine and fertility and the inspiration for Greek theater. In the sixth century B.C., on the eastern slope of the Acropolis, just below the Parthenon, the world's first theater was constructed in tribute to the wine-god. Dionysus also inspired many festivals and was one of the most beloved habitues of Mt. Olympus.

Wine and the Birth of Theater

The Greeks gave birth to theater, and the original Greek dramatists were all celebrants of the Dionysian spirit:

Aeschylus (525 B.C.-456 B.C.)The author of *Agamemnon, Prometheus Bound* and *Oresteia*. Aeschylus is considered to be the originator of Greek tragedy. He was a brilliant innovator—the first to integrate the chorus into the plot of a play and to put multiple actors on the stage. Prior to Aeschylus, most theater featured a single performer who played different roles with the help of masks, as the chorus chanted in the background.

Aeschylus attributed his success as a playwright to a dream he had as a child, a dream inspired by a day of watching grapes ripen in the vineyards. He explains that the god of wine appeared to him and commanded him to write tragic plays, and he thus began writing that very morning. For Aeschylus, wine is a muse and a catalyst in the development of self-knowledge. He observed, "Wine is the mirror of the mind."

Euripides (c. 485 - 406 B.C) Another innovative dramatist, Euripides introduced women as performers on the stage and satirized the foibles of the gods. In *The Bacchae*, Euripides pays homage to wine: "Mankind . . . possesses two supreme blessings. First of these is the goddess Demeter, or Earth ... It was she who gave to man his nourishment of grain. But after her there came the son of Semele, who matched her present by inventing liquid wine as his gift to man. For filled with that good gift, suffering mankind forgets its grief; from it comes sleep;

with it oblivion of the troubles of the day. There is no other medicine for misery."

In an expression of his egalitarian sentiments, Euripides writes, "To rich and poor alike he hath granted the delight of wine, that makes all pain to cease." He adds, "Where there is no wine there is no love."

Aristophanes (c. 448-385 B.C.) The playwright and poet Aristophanes, author of *The Clouds* opined, " …'tis when men drink they thrive—Grow wealthy, speed their business, win their suits, make themselves happy, benefit their friends."

Aristophanes adds, "Quickly, bring me a beaker of wine, so that I may wet my mind and say something clever."

Wine: Inspiration for the Muses
"Bacchus opens the gate of the heart."
—Homer

The Greek gods were a very dramatic, theatrical cast of characters. They were tempestuous, creative, jealous, and sex-crazed. In addition to his sortie with Semele, Zeus also made love with the goddess of perfect memory, Mnemosyne, for nine days and nights continuously. The result of the confluence of unlimited energy (Zeus) and eternal memory (Mnemosyne) was the birth of the nine Muses, including the goddesses of poetry, dance, painting, music, and sculpture. (The word museum means "house of the muses.")

The muse of sculpture clearly inspired the original bronze masterpiece *Perseus* by the great Renaissance master Benevenuto Cellini (1500-1571). On display in the Piazza in front of the Palazzo Vecchio in Florence, Perseus holds the recently severed head of the gorgon Medusa. According to the ancient Greeks her blood formed a fertile crimson stream from which the mighty winged steed Pegasus emerged. Bridled with gold by Athena, the matron goddess of Athens, Pegasus carried the hero Bellerophon, who slew the hideous monster Chimera.

After the battle, Pegasus flew to Mount Helicon. As he landed his hooves clipped the mountain's peak, releasing the flow of the divine spring within. The Helicon Spring irrigated the vineyards below and made possible the cultivation of wine. This became the wine of the Muses and the source of their creative inspiration.

According to Charles Freeman, author of *The Greek Achievement*, the Greeks generated the creative inspiration for Western civilization. He proclaims, "The Greeks provided the chromosomes of Western Civilization." And those wine-soaked chromosomes were "sequenced" by the seminal figures of Western philosophy, Socrates (469–399 B.C) and Plato (Circa 428-348 B .C.).

The Original Symposium

*"Nothing more excellent or valuable than wine
was ever granted by the Gods to man."*
— Plato

The forum for the birth of Western philosophy was a delightful gathering known as the Symposium. "Symposium" literally means "to drink together." The participants, all men from noble families, wore togas and floral garlands as they reclined on cushioned couches next to low tables upon which servants placed beautifully decorated cups and jugs of wine. After dining, the group of between twelve and thirty participants engaged in a carefully programmed ritual of drinking and philosophical discussion. The gatherings also featured poetry, jokes, and music. For Socrates, Plato, and their associates, the Symposium presented an opportunity to heighten intellectual and spiritual awareness in an enjoyable and convivial manner.

Plato's famous dialogue *The Symposium* was focused on an exploration of the true meaning of love. But it begins with a discussion of how much wine to drink: "Socrates took his place on the couch, and supped with the rest; and then libations were offered, and after a hymn had been sung to the gods, and there had been the usual ceremonies, they were about to commence drinking, when Pausanias said: 'And now, my friends, how can we drink with least injury to ourselves? I can assure you that I feel severely the effect of yesterday's potations, and must have time to recover, and I suspect that most of you are in the same predicament, for you were of the party yesterday. Consider then: How. can the drinking be made easiest?' "

Although Socrates' most famous drink was his last, he was renowned in happier times as the Symposium's most prodigious consumer of wine. Plato recounts that his teacher could drink more than any one else without showing any effects whatsoever.

"Socrates' approach to drinking wine expressed his earthy and realistic philosophy," notes Ron Gross, author of *Socrates Way*. Gross explains, "He used it pleasurably and prudently, to stimulate the flow of good conversation. His self-control while imbibing was a practical demonstration of his belief in the importance of moderation. For Socrates, wine lubricated his wit and sharpened his insights, so that he could listen more critically and express himself more precisely."

Socrates said, "Wine moistens and tempers the spirits, and lulls the cares of the mind to rest…it revives our joys, and is oil to the dying flame of life. If we drink temperately, and small draughts at a time, the wine distills into our lungs like sweetest morning dew…It is then that the wine commits no rape upon our reason, but pleasantly invites us to agreeable mirth."

In addition to counseling moderation, Socrates also suggested that wine helped to liberate the intuition and the poetic soul. He observed: "I decided that it was not wisdom that enabled poets to write their poetry, but a kind of instinct or inspiration, such as you find in seers and prophets who deliver all their sublime messages without knowing in the least what they mean."

Plato, Socrates' greatest student, created the model of elementary, secondary, and university education that we still employ today. He laid the framework for our system of intellectual inquiry, logic, and debate in the quest for understanding truth, beauty and goodness. Plato believed that the knowledge of truth, beauty, and goodness was held deep within the soul and that the role of the teacher was *to draw forth* this innate wisdom. Wine was an integral part of the philosopher's approach and was shared in moderate proportion by the master and his students at the end of each day at his original Academy. Plato stated that wine was offered to mankind "in order to implant modesty in the soul and health and strength in the body."

Plato believed that the enjoyment of wine became more important as the years passed. He explains that wine is "the cure for the crabbedness of old age, whereby we may renew our youth and enjoy forgetfulness of despair."

The Symposium was a living expression of Plato's advice, "Life must be lived as play." He understood the role of wine in facilitating a more playful and open attitude. He noted, "You can learn more about a man in an hour of play than in a year of conversation."

Play wasn't frivolous for Plato. He believed that wine-induced relaxation and the resultant flow of mirth served as a mirror for character. He wrote, "What is better adapted than the festive use of wine, in the first place to test, and in the second place to train the character of a man, if care be taken in the use of it.? What is there cheaper or more innocent?"

Beyond Retsina

Four thousand years ago, Greece led the world in wine production and trade. Greek wine was shipped in *amphorae (amphi* is ancient Greek for "on both sides" and phero is "to carry") These pottery wine vessels had two handles and a neck much narrower than the body. Amphorae were sealed with stoppers made of pinewood and pine resin, and the resin imparted a characteristic flavor. Even after more sophisticated means evolved for sealing the vessels, many Greek wines were resinated intentionally. This became known as retsina but this flavor didn't resonate with contemporary taste, and it led to a diminishing reputation for Greek wine. In the last quarter century, Greece is making a comeback. With more than two hundred indigenous grape varieties, a superb wine-growing climate and a huge infusion of investment and modern technology, Greece is poised to be a wine region to watch over the next twenty-five years. Look for wines imported by Sotiris Bafitis Selections. (www.sotirisbafitis.com)

The Renaissance: "Diwine" Comedy

Renaissance means "rebirth," specifically, the rebirth of ancient clasical notions of individual human potential and creativity. The great figures who contributed to this extraordinary transformation of consciousness, from Dante to Galileo, all loved wine and all paid tribute to the genius of Greece and Rome. When the Byzantine Empire fell in 1453, scholars streamed into Italy from Constantinople, bringing with them manuscripts in ancient Greek and Latin. This influx of intellectual capital serendipitously coincided with the increasing availability of the innovative new printing press, and the resulting explosion of knowledge transformed the consciousness of the Western world. Among the writings that became particularly popular were the works of the great Roman poets Ovid, Virgil and Horace, all of whom paid tribute to the divine juice of the grape.

Ovid, Virgil and Horace

The greatest poets of ancient Rome all wrote about and were inspired by wine.

Ovid (43 BC – 17 AD) Ovid, author of *The Metamorphoses* and *The Art of Love* set the stage for much of the poetry of the Middle Ages and has had an enduring influence in the literature and art of the Western world. Ovid brings to life many of the original Greek myths, including the story of Bacchus and Ariadne. He noted," Wine rouses courage and makes men more apt for passion." He adds, "When there is plenty of wine, sorrow and worry take wing."

Virgil (70 B.C-19 B.C) Author of the *Aeneid*, an epic poem inspired by Homer, Virgil is considered to be the greatest of the Roman poets. Virgil serves as Dante's tour guide in *The Divine Comedy*. In the *Aeneid*, he refers to wine, vineyards and Bacchus frequently. His characters "restore their strength with meat and cheer their souls with wine," and honor the gods by pouring drops of wine on the ground before drinking deeply.

Virgil describes a wine-tasting event in Chapter 8:

> *"Fill high the goblets with a sparkling flood,*
> *And with deep draughts invoke our common god."*

But, although the epic recounts far more mayhem than merriment, Virgil reminds us in a previous chapter to toast to the present moment:

> *"Crown high the goblets with a cheerful draught;*
> *Enjoy the present hour; adjourn the future thought."*

Horace (65 – 8, B.C.) was Emperor Augustus' favorite poet.

He wrote:

> *"Wine brings to light the hidden secrets of the soul,*
> *Gives being to our hopes,*
> *Bids the coward fight, drives dull care away,*
> *And teaches new means for the accomplishment*
> *of our wishes.*

Renaissance Superstars

When the Screaming Eagle winery released their first Cabernet Sauvignon in 1992 it sold for $50. If you can find a bottle today you'll pay between $7,000 to $27,000! Screaming Eagle is the most egregious example of the modern "cult wine." The original "cult wine" was grown on the slopes of Mount Falernus just south of Naples. Falernian was hailed as the greatest wine of Roman times. The Falernian vintage of 121 B.C. was especially prized by connoisseurs of the day and became so expensive that only the emperor could afford it. The Romans continued to cultivate vineyards and to produce fine wine until the demise of the Empire. In his classic work *The History of the Decline and Fall of the Roman Empire*, English historian Edward Gibbon (1737-1794) proposed 476 (A.D.) as the official date for the fall of Rome.

What were the great scientific and technological breakthroughs in Europe from that date until the dawn of the Renaissance? According to American historian William Manchester (1922-2004), author of *A World Lit Only by Fire*, there weren't many. Other than the windmill and the water wheel, Europe's main innovations consisted of increasingly clever torture machines to dissuade anyone from questioning church doctrine.

The Middle or "Dark" Age in Europe was an unsanitary, plague-ridden, violent, and remarkably backward time. In the thousand years prior to the Renaissance, our contemporary notions of individuality, self-expression, and creativity didn't exist. The great art historian Sir Kenneth Clark (1903-1983), explains, "The discovery of the individual was made in early fifteenth century Florence." In the Middle Ages artists were anonymous, as were winemakers. As the Renaissance blossomed, individuals like Brunelleschi, Leonardo, and Michelangelo not only signed their works, they became superstars. At the same time, great winemakers like Antinori, Frescobaldi, and Mazzei launched the vinous dynasties that still reign today.

Renaissance Wine-Makers

Giovanni di Piero Antinori joined the Florentine Guild of Vintners in May, 1385. Subsequent generations of the family became closely linked to the Medici as silk traders, bankers and wine makers. In 1498, as a member of the city council, Tommaso Antinori voted to condemn the heretical monk Savonarola- who strove zealously to remove all the dolce from Florentine vita- to be burned at the stake in the town square. (Savonarola was the force behind the infamous "Bonfire of the Vanities" in which the works of Botticelli and other "decadent" artists were consigned to the flames. Ultimately, Savonarola's fanaticism, and his open criticism of the Pope, led to his becoming the centerpiece of his own bonfire.) Tommaso's sons Niccolo', Carlo, Lodovico, and Raffaello developed the family's wine production and made the type of wine that Michelangelo requested when he was away from his hometown. (www.antinori.it -wines include Tignanello, Solaia, Badia a Passignano)

In the beginning of the fourteenth century, Florentine banker Berto de Frescobaldi bequeathed his vineyards, orchards and farms to his children. They began to produce wines there and by the time of the Renaissance they were providing vino for a number of popes, artists and kings. Their clients included England's Henry VIII and artists such as Donatello and Michelozzo Michelozzi.(www.frescobaldi.it-wines include Giramonte, Castel Giocondo, Montesodi)

Like Leonardo daVinci's father, Ser Lapo Mazzei (1350-1412), was a notary of the Florence city government. He also spawned a tradition of making fine wine. In 1394, Lapo writes to the wealthy merchant of Prato, Francesco Datini, "Don't concern yourself about the cost of the wine, though it be high: its goodness is restorative." On December 16, 1398, according to the Datini family archives Ser Lapo Mazzei introduced the name Chianti in an invoice for six barrels of wine. (www.mazzei.it Wines include Castello di Fonterutoli, Belguardo, Siepi)

The Juice of Genius

Wine served as the muse for many of the great figures of the Renaissance. Dante Alighieri (1265-1321) the great Florentine poet, wrote *The Divine Comedy*, one of the world's literary masterpieces. Originally entitled *La Commedia* it was dubbed "Divine" by his first biographer, Giovanni Boccaccio (1313-1375). Revered in Italy as "The Supreme Poet," Dante is also considered to be the patriarch of *la bella lingua*, the beautiful Italian language.

In *The Divine Comedy*, Dante mentions the wine of Vernaccia, but the context is a cautionary one for the connoisseur: An unfortunate pope finds himself in the *Inferno's* "Terrace of Gluttony" for overindulging in Bolsena eels cooked in Vernaccia wine.

Hope for the Pope

Formalized in the sixth century by Pope Gregory the Great, the seven deadly sins are featured throughout *The Divine Comedy*. A few years ago, a group of French chefs and intellectuals led by the great Paul Bocuse sent a petition to the pope, asking him to reclassify the fifth deadly sin, gluttony.

The French word for gluttony is *gourmandise*, and Bocuse and his colleagues explain that the word has evolved over the years to refer to one who savors good food and fine wine. Bocuse explains, "To be a gourmand is one of life's great pleasures. Gourmands don't just appreciate fine food and good wine, but they share it - and thus double the pleasure."

Gluttony is mindless overindulgence. Appreciating wonderful food and wine with reverence and gratitude is *paradisio* on earth.

Exiled from Florence for political reasons, Dante arrived in Verona in 1312, where he lived under the patronage of a wealthy family. In 1353 Dante's son Pietro Alighieri purchased vineyards and a villa in the hills of Valpolicella, an area known as Vaio Armaron. This proved to be a wise investment, as the robust, fragrant wines from this region have been acclaimed since antiquity. Dante's direct descendant Count Pieralvise Serego Alighieri continues to make wine there today in partnership with the Masi Estate.

An ardent admirer of Dante, the Marchesi Fernando Frescobaldi is a charming ambassador for his family's legendary winery. At a recent tasting of some of their greatest wines in Florence, Fernando, with an extra twinkle in his eye, shared the following story. "One of my ancestors, Dino Frescobaldi, was a poet and a friend of a young, aspiring writer. His name was Dante Aligheri. One day, Dante expressed his frustration with his grand undertaking. He said to Dino, 'What the hell am I doing?' My ancestor poured him some good wine and offered encouraging words, telling the fledging author to 'keep on writing'."

Dante's contribution to the Italian language helped set the stage for the Renaissance.

Another wine lover, Filippo Brunelleschi, (1377-1446) became the inspiration for the great achievements of Leonardo, Michelangelo and many others. The first art historian, Giorgio Vasari, author of *The Lives of the Artists,* proclaimed, "Brunelleschi's genius was so commanding that we can surely say that he was sent by heaven to renew the art of architecture." Brunelleschi discovered the application of three-dimensional perspective and taught it to his friends Masaccio, who created the first Renaissance painting, and Donatello, who completed the first Renaissance sculpture. Then, Brunelleschi designed and constructed the magnificent dome of the Florence cathedral, thereby altering our concept of space, and ourselves, forever.

Brunelleschi translated his remarkable vision into practical accomplishment by managing his workforce of masons, carpenters, and laborers for twenty-six years. As a manager he realized that it wasn't efficient for his crew to come down from the scaffolding, 180 feet above ground, to use the lavatory or to break for lunch. Brunelleschi constructed sanitary facilities in the sky and invited his associates to enjoy lunch from their perch above the city. And he offered wine to his workforce.

Ross King, author of *Brunelleschi's Dome: How a Renaissance Genius Reinvented Architecture,* explains: "To slake their thirst on sweltering summer days the workers drank wine…Strange and inadvisable as a draft of wine might seem under these circumstances…wine was a healthier drink than water…And the Florentines placed great faith in the wholesome properties of wine. Drunk in moderation it was said to improve the blood, hasten digestion, calm the intellect, enliven the spirit, and expel wind. It might also have given a fillip of courage to men clinging to an inward-curving vault several hundred feet above the ground."

As a young man in Florence, Leonardo da Vinci visited the Brancacci Chapel, where he was inspired by the use of perspective in the frescoes of Brunelleschi's student Masaccio. And many believe that it was the young Leonardo himself who served as the model for Donatello's David, hailed as the first Renaissance sculpture.

Leonardo's notebooks refer to "wine, the divine juice of the grape." He included wine on the shopping lists that he sometimes jotted in the margins of his notebooks, and he usually enjoyed a glass or two of red wine with dinner. Leonardo was a pioneer in botany and did many detailed studies of the formation and structure of the vine. He invented new, more efficient wine presses and owned a vineyard that was given to him by the Duke of Milan in lieu of the money he was due for services rendered to the Sforza court.

Most of Leonardo's notes about wine focus on counsels of moderation. He cautions against overindulgence and drunkenness: " When wine is drunk by a drunkard, that wine is revenged on the drinker."

Leonardo painted a Bacchus that was originally intended to be a portrayal of St. John in the desert. Scholars believe that an unknown seventeenth-century painter added the cluster of grapes and other traditional symbols associated with the wine-god, but Leonardo's mysterious sfumato technique, the use of countless gossamer-thin layers of paint and an intentional blurring of edges, and the unusual pose in which the maestro places his figure, all suggest the spirit of Bacchus.

The Leonardo Da Vinci winery in Tuscany makes a Chianti Classico and a Brunello di Montalcino named in honor of the maestro. www.davinciwine.com

Twenty-three years younger than Leonardo, Michelangelo Buonarroti (1475-1564) was hailed as "divine" by his contemporaries. Professor William Wallace, Chairman of the Department of the History of Art at Washington University, points out, "Michelangelo Buonarroti loved wine. When he was working in Bologna he always sent for the wine of his native Tuscany." Wallace notes that Michelangelo complained, "The Bolognese drink lousy wine." The same was

Leonardo's *Bacchus*

true when he labored in Rome, as Wallace explains, "Although the artist's Roman house had a fig tree and grape vines, he nonetheless appreciated the quality produce sent (by his nephew) from Florence: approximately forty flasks of Trebbiano wine every June, a dozen or more marzolino cheeses sent each winter, and, more sporadically, fruit — mostly pears and apples — as well as other specialty items such as peas, chick peas, Tuscan beans, sausage, and ravioli."

Before the creation of his miraculous *Pieta* the young genius was given a large block of marble by Cardinal Riario from Rome who effectively challenged the precocious Florentine, "See what you can do with this."

What did Michelangelo choose as his subject? Bacchus, god of wine.

Now in Florence's Bargello Museum, Michelangelo's Bacchus is an early masterpiece (1496-98). Professor Wallace described it at a seminar in Florence entitled "In the Footsteps of Michelangelo," "This sculpture is more pagan than classical. It's intoxicating in a way you will soon discover." Wallace explains, "Michelangelo understood that the ancients drank wine for inspiration, for insight. He makes his figure somewhat bleary-eyed and stumbling, yet graceful."

The figure is designed so that one is compelled to walk around it in circles. Wallace emphasizes, "Michelangelo makes him interesting from all angles, with an especially great butt. The more we circulate the dizzier and more intoxicated we get."

Michelangelo places a mischievous faun near the base. The sprite is nibbling away at Bacchus's cluster of grapes. We view the work with our heads well above the faun but below the level of the god. Wallace explains that the work is "both serious and humorous. Michelangelo brings us some humor as a touch of the divine. And, as we complete our circumambulation of the statue we become aware that the god is eyeing us sharply

Michelangelo's *Bacchus*

through the handle of his wine-cup," as if to ask if we are opening to his spirit, to creative, wine-inspired insight.

Although stories of the rivalry between Michelangelo and Leonardo are probably exaggerated, we do know that they were each commissioned by the Florentine government to paint opposite walls in the Grand Council Hall of the Palazzo Vecchio. Leonardo, already renowned as a supreme master, was asked to commemorate the Battle of Anghiari, while the precocious Michaelangelo was engaged to paint the Battle of Cascina. The Florentine city fathers hoped to inspire the competitive instincts of both men to generate ultimate master works. Although this vision was never realized (Leonardo tried an experiment for drying his paint that failed and Michelangelo, after completing some preparatory sketches, was called away by a more important client, Pope Julius II), art historian Kenneth Clark emphasizes: "The battle cartoons of Leonardo and Michelangelo are the turning point of the Renaissance…they initiate the two styles which sixteenth century painting was to develop, the Baroque and Classical." Who was the primary influence in arranging these world-changing commissions? Niccolo Machiavelli (1469-1527)!

Machiavelli, author of *The Prince* and *The Discourses,* is the innovator who brought the *science* into *political science.* The father of modern political theory and the originator of "realpolitik," Machiavelli noted, "Men will not look at things as they really are, but as they wish them to be—and are ruined." Machiavelli loved good wine, and the elixir of genius is ever present throughout his career. He inherited vineyards from his father as well as a life-long love for reading and learning.

In his superb biography, *Machiavelli: Philosopher of Power,* Ross King explains that Niccolo's father, Bernardo, had an extraordinary passion for reading: "His formal education would have seen him studying Latin grammar, perfecting his handwriting, and learning how to compose wills and certify business and marriage contracts. His mind roved more broadly and searchingly over human affairs than such paperwork allowed, and by the 1470s he was dabbling in classical literature." King notes that among Bernardo's most prized possessions was an edition of Livy's *History of Rome.* King explains that in 1486, "he had the work bound in leather, a task for which he compensated the binder with three bottles of red wine from his estate in the country."

Bernardo passed the book along to his son, and it proved to be a major inspiration. Many scholars consider Niccolo Machiavelli's greatest and most influential work to be the *Discourses on the First Ten Decades of Livy.* This masterpiece was a profound influence on the Founding Fathers of the United States. "And so," Ross King muses, "perhaps life, liberty, and the pursuit of happiness can ultimately be traced back to those three bottles of red from the Machiavelli estate?"

King also notes that Machiavelli often used Tuscan wine as a gift on diplomatic missions, such as his visit to the notorious Cesare Borgia in Imola in 1502. Borgia is, of course, one of the central figures of

The Prince, which Machiavelli would write a decade later. King surmises, "we can see the two men sitting down and discussing politics over a glass or two of Frescobaldi wine."

While preparing for his diplomatic encounter with Borgia, Machiavelli wrote to his associate in Florence requesting a velvet-and-damask cloak and a new velvet hat (evidently he wished to cut a better appearance at Borgia's court) and a shipment of fine Tuscan wine. Machiavelli's associates in Florence weren't always accommodating, however, and in one particularly memorable note he was told: "Go scratch your ass. You can go to the devil for asking so many things."

When the government of Florence sent Machiavelli into exile, he spent much of his time overseeing his vineyards and making a wine known as Vermiglio, a predecessor of modern Chianti. About four hundred years ago, the Machiavelli family vineyards just outside Florence passed through marriage to another family, and they produce wines there to this day. Look for the Antica Fattoria Machiavelli Chianti Classico.

Machiavelli, like Michelangelo and to some extent Leonardo, relied throughout much of his career on the patronage of the Medici. And it was the Medici who also sponsored the work of another great Renaissance figure, Galileo Galilei (1564-1642).

Dava Sobel, author of the *New York Times* bestseller *Galileo's Daughter: A Historical Memoir of Science, Faith, and Love* confirms that wine was an inspiration to the man who many agree was the father of modern science. Galileo referred to wine poetically as "light held together by moisture."

Sobel comments that Galileo's daughter, Suor Maria Celeste, wrote her father a number of letters imploring him to moderate his consumption. But Galileo remained under the sway of Bacchus. Sobel jokes, "Oh, to have lived when wine was considered the safer alternative to water!"

James Beard award-winning chef Roberto Donna opened his Galileo and Laboratorio di Galileo restaurants in Washington, D.C.

more than twenty years ago. With a wine list recognized by a *Wine Spectator* Grand Award of Excellence, Galileo was also named one of the twenty finest Italian restaurants in the world by the president of Italy. Donna comments on why he chose to name his establishments after Galileo: "Galileo always inspired me. He was my childhood hero. I opened my restaurant in a very artistic, multi-cultural neighborhood, and my vision was to inspire my customers with the genius inherent in the Italian tradition of food and wine. I knew that Galileo loved wine and that he was ahead of his time in so many ways. Just as he looked beyond the limitations of the world view of most of his contemporaries I wished to launch a new pioneering concept for fine Italian cuisine, combining the best of tradition with an experimental approach. Galileo wrote, 'In the discussion of natural problems we ought to begin not with the scriptures, but with experiments, and demonstrations.' The same is true with cooking and enjoying wine."

The Medici

The Medici provided the funding for the development of the great art and science of the Renaissance, as well as many of the great Italian wine dynasties. The family invited the leading figures of the Renaissance to share wine, poetry and conversation at their estate. Brunelleschi, Leonardo, Michelangelo, Raphael, and many others attended the Medici version of the Symposium.

Caterina de' Medici (1519-1589) is one of the most influential figures in the history of food and wine. At age fourteen, this great-granddaughter of Lorenzo the Magnificent was betrothed to the future king of France, Henry of Orlèans, the second son of Leonardo da Vinci's great patron, King Francois I. In addition to introducing the high-heeled shoe and the art of ballet to the French, Caterina brought the ingredients and secrets of Italian cooking to France, including pasta, artichokes, peas, white beans, duck in orange sauce, onion soup, sorbets, ice cream, and fine pastry. French *haute cuisine* was effectively launched by this extraordinary Italian woman.

Caterina introduced Florentine elegance in the form of gracious table settings, exquisitely embroidered tablecloths and napkins, wine glasses, and fine silverware (the French still ate with their fingers until Caterina introduced the fork). Prior to Caterina, meat, fish and sweets were all eaten at once in medieval style, but she created the modern protocol of a progression in a meal from a fish course (with white wine) to meat and other savories (with red wine), finishing with dessert (with sweet wine). Salud!

The Founding Fathers: America's First Wine Geeks

The notion of individuality was reborn in the Renaissance. In the Age of Enlightenment, philosophers like Francis Bacon (1561 – 1626), Baruch Spinoza (1632–1672) and Voltaire 1694 –1778) developed the ideal of universal human rights and individual freedom. But in the late eighteenth century, England and France were still ruled by kings. China and Japan were controlled by "heavenly" emperors. Russia was the dominion of an imperial tsar, and Turkey was subject to an all-powerful sultan. The Declaration of Independence on July 4, 1776, and the adoption of the United States Constitution on September 17, 1787, represented the first time in human history that the rights of the individual were enshrined in the founding charter of a nation.

When the Constitution was ratified the delegates threw a party in Philadelphia. They toasted the new republic with sixty bottles of Bordeaux, fifty-four bottles of beer and bowls of punch so big that, according to wine historian James Gabler, "ducks could swim in them." Like the ancient Greeks and the geniuses of the Renaissance, the founding fathers loved wine.

First among those founding fathers was the extraordinary Renaissance Man Benjamin Franklin (1706-1790). Renowned as a multifaceted genius, Franklin was a scientist, inventor, diplomat, author, and wine connoisseur. His personal wine cellar was filled with more than 1,100 bottles, featuring the finest examples of Champagne, Burgundy, and Bordeaux.

Franklin believed that wine was good for both physical and emotional health. He wrote, "Wine makes daily living easier, less hurried, with fewer tensions and more tolerance."

Wine: The Blessing of Providence

"Because I would have every man make advantage of the Blessings of Providence, and few are aquainted with the method of making wine of the grapes which grow wild in our woods, I do here present them with a few easy directions, drawn from some years experience, which, if they will follow, they may furnish themselves with a wholesome sprightly Claret which will keep for several years and is not inferior to that which passeth for French Claret."

—Opening paragraph of Benjamin Franklin's guide to winemaking from *Poor Richard's Almanack*, 1743

For Franklin, wine was an everyday miracle. As he expressed it: "We hear of the conversion of water into wine at the marriage in Cana as a miracle. But this conversion is, through the goodness of God, made every day before our eyes. Behold the rain which descends from heaven upon our vineyards, and which incorporates itself with the grapes, to be changed into wine; a constant proof that God loves us, and loves to see us happy."

By the time he served as American Minister to France, Franklin was a living legend. His *savoir faire* and knowledge of fine wine allowed him to set the stage for French support of the fledging American experiment.

Benjamin Franklin was the embodiment of *joie de vivre*, but it took a man with a much more stoic temperament to lead the new Republic to success in battle. Although George Washington (1732-1799), the first president of the United States, wasn't particularly a *bon vivant*, he felt that wine was an essential element of life. He noted, "My manner of living is plain, a glass of wine and a bit of mutton are always ready, and such as will be content to partake of that are always welcome."

Washington appointed Thomas Jefferson as Secretary of State and chief wine consultant. Jefferson advised the president on the challenges of dealing with the Barbary pirates who raided American vessels and, as James Gabler points out in *Passions: The Wines and Travels of Thomas Jefferson*, "As Washington's Secretary of State, Jefferson was guiding the chief executive through other perilous foreign waters-ordering French wines." The archives of the esteemed Chateau d'Yquem record that Jefferson ordered thirty cases of the precious Sauternes for the first Commander-in-Chief. Washington also particularly enjoyed Champagne and Jefferson helped him stock his cellar with the best.

Washington's successor, John Adams (1735-1826) is renowned as the "Atlas of Independence." His intellect, patriotism and statesmanship were vital to the founding of the United States. James Gabler refers to the second president of the United States as "an enthusiastic wine drinker," and notes that, "dinner at the Adamses' was always accompanied or followed by wine."

During his diplomatic tenure in Paris, Adams developed a taste for the finest Bordeaux, and he accumulated an impressive collection. Just prior to his appointment as America's first ambassador to Britain, he placed an order for five hundred bottles of fine French wine. But when he discovered that his diplomatic status didn't provide immunity from the excessive duty charged by the British for each bottle brought into the country, he appealed to his friend Thomas Jefferson to help reduce the shipment.

In the spring of 1777, Adams bemoaned the temporary lack of

availability of some of his favorite wines due to problems with shipping. He wrote to his wife Abigail, "Wine is not to be had under sixty-eight dollars per gallon, and that very bad. ... In short, I am getting nothing that I can drink, and I believe I shall be sick from this cause alone."

Of all the founding fathers, Thomas Jefferson (1743-1826) was the most knowledgeable about wine. Franklin, Washington, Adams, Madison and Monroe all appreciated Bordeaux, Burgundy, and other fine wines, but it was Jefferson who took the lead in connoisseurship and in helping to obtain the best wines for his friends. In addition to serving as wine consultant for Washington and Adams, Jefferson also advised James Monroe when he was elected president in 1817. His congratulatory letter to Monroe focuses primarily on recommendations for the presidential cellar. Jefferson wrote, "I shall not waste your time on idle congratulations. You know my joy on the commitment of the helm of government to your hands. I promised you, when I should have received and tried the wines that I ordered from France and Italy, to give you a note of the kinds which I should think worthy of your procurement...I now fulfill my promise..."

Dolley: Décolletage, Delicacies and Diplomacy

Dolley Madison (1768-1849) served as hostess for Thomas Jefferson during his two terms in office, and then became known as the first first lady when her husband James became president. She also organized and facilitated the first inaugural ball in 1809.

Dolley enjoyed and appreciated fine wine, especially Champagne. Her husband suggested that she moderate her consumption of bubbly because, "If you drink much of it, it will make you hop like the cork."

Dolley brought an exceptional level of social intelligence to her role as hostess. As Henry Clay once exclaimed at one her parties, "Everybody loves Mrs. Madison!" Dolley responded,

"That's because Mrs. Madison loves everybody!"

Renowned for her ability to remember names and faces, Dolley had the gift of making everyone feel special. She brought *joie de vivre* to the social scene of the emerging republic. Her dinners always featured the finest wines served with exceptional delicacies prepared by her French chef. Dolley's sweet tooth led her to serve lots of ice cream, cookies, and other treats for dessert. She often wrapped little packages of dried fruits and nuts for her guests and wrote poems on bits of paper that she tucked inside.

Although Dolley's decolletage drew more attention than her diplomacy, both Jefferson and her husband valued her political acumen. Her charm and grace helped to defuse combustible situations and set the stage for diplomatic progress. During the dark days of the War of 1812, she used her social gifts to maintain morale. On a very practical note, she rescued the original draft of the Constitution and the Declaration of Independence, along with Stuart's portrait of George Washington, from the invading British troops who burned the White House.

The third president of the United States, Jefferson was, like Franklin, an extraordinary Renaissance Man. The author of the Declaration of Independence and the founder of the University of Virginia, Jefferson was an architect, inventor, musician, and philosopher. Thomas Jefferson was also, as Jay McInerney, author of *A Hedonist in the Cellar: Adventures in Wine,* calls him, " the founding wine geek."

When he succeeded Franklin as the official American Minister to France in1787, Jefferson took the opportunity to travel throughout the country. His itinerary featured extensive visits to all the best wine regions. Jefferson purchased large quantities of the finest Bordeaux, including Lafitte, Margaux, Haut Brion, and D'Yquem and great

Montrachets, Chambertins, Vosnes, and Volnays from Burgundy. In 1801 Jefferson received a salary of $25,000. He spent more than 20 percent of it on fine wine.

Jefferson understood the power of wine to inspire creative thinking and bring people together. Fine wine and its appreciation were always featured at the dinners he held for his cabinet and for visiting dignitaries. As James Gabler recounts, Jefferson, "...discovered that fine wines and food were a great way to meet informally with his political friends and foes, never talking politics, but dropping a hint here and there of how he felt on a subject."

Jefferson wrote, "Good wine is a necessity of life for me." He understood that wine was a civilizing and healthy influence, and he did his best to launch a culture of wine in the new republic. He emphasized, "I think it is a great error to consider a heavy tax on wines as a tax on luxury. On the contrary, it is a tax on the health of our citizens."

Jefferson brought European wine makers to the United States, including Filippo Mazzei, the direct ancestor of today's Mazzei family, producers of some of Italy's finest wines. Although their initial efforts to cultivate vineyards and produce great wines fell short, Jefferson's vinous vision has ultimately been realized. He noted, "Wine being among the earliest luxuries in which we indulge ourselves; it is desirable that it should be made here and we have every soil, aspect, and climate of the best wine countries."

Jefferson's Vinous Vision

The Virginia wine industry began when George Washington and George Mason invested in the four hundred-acre vineyard project conceived by Thomas Jefferson and Filippo Mazzei in 1773. Although the War of Independence interfered with the realization of their plans, the original notion has come to fruition two hundred years later. Today, Jefferson Vineyards produces a delightful range of wines on the original property staked out by Mazzei and Jefferson. Virginia is now home to more than 130 wineries, including the highly acclaimed Barboursville Vineyards, Horton Cellars, Oakencroft Vineyard & Winery, and Rappahannock Cellars.

The Art of Wine

The world of wine attracts its share of snobs, but they are just a drop in the spit bucket compared with the profusion of art snobs. Events at art galleries often include wine tastings so one can have the opportunity to experience the worst of both worlds. At an art gallery wine-event in New York City, I recently heard a fellow, clad in tight black jeans and a black turtleneck, describe some indecipherable markings on a huge mostly empty canvas by proclaiming, in what seemed like a fake British accent, "Of course it's not actually *trompe l'oeil*, it's more of a post-modern interior conversation." He punctuated this proclamation with a perfunctory sip of his Chardonnay.

For the enlightened connoisseur of wine or art, appreciation isn't a function of the ego. Rather, it's an experience of opening to something greater than one's self. Sergio Esposito, author of *Passion on the Vine*, writes about the experience of fine wine in a way that touches the essence of appreciating all great art: "Its value lies in the fact that you can never understand or master it. To begin to see even a small portion of what it is, you must smother your ego, stop trying to win at some mad game, and let yourself become completely engulfed by something bigger than you."

We can taste the essence of sun and earth in a great wine, and enjoy an experience of communion with the source of its creation. Like a fine wine, a great painting invites us to see the world, and perhaps our selves, in a new way. As we suspend our preconceptions and allow ourselves to be moved by the brushstrokes on a canvas, we may feel the pure impulse of the artist's inspiration.

Wine has inspired artists through the ages. Admittedly, much wine-inspired art is banal and tasteless. Yet Bacchus has also brought out the best in artists over the centuries. Let's enjoy a taste of some of the finest wine-inspired painting.

Bacchus in Paint

"Wine awakens and refreshes the lurking passions of the mind, as
varnish does the colors which are sunk in a picture, and brings
them out in all their natural glowings."
—Alexander Pope (1688-1744), English poet

In his *Treatise on Painting*, Leonardo da Vinci makes his case for painting as first among the arts. He explains, "The painter is master of all the things that can befall the mind of man, and therefore if he wishes to see beauties that would enrapture him, he is master of their production." Leonardo believed that painting was superior to sculpture. He argued, "Painting involves greater mental deliberation and is of greater artifice and wonder than sculpture, in that necessity requires the mind of the painter to transmute itself into nature's own mind."

Of the innumerable wine-inspired paintings, the following represent my list of those that inspire the greatest rapture, wonder and delight.

Titian (Tiziano Vecello) (1485- 1576) *Bacchus and Ariadne* (1520-23), National Gallery, London (oil on canvas)

Titian is the rock star of sixteenth century Venetian painters. His fans included Emperor Charles V and his son King Philip II of Spain, Pope Paul III, and the great patron of Leonardo da Vinci, Francis I, King of France.

Based on the tales of Ovid, this magnificent painting captures the moment that Bacchus, god of wine, falls in love, at first sight, with Princess Ariadne. Ariadne had been in love with Theseus (she helped him slay the pesky Minotaur on the island of Crete). But as she napped on the island of Naxos after their adventure, Theseus took off, never to return. Ovid describes Ariadne as, "clad in an ungirt tunic, barefoot, golden hair unbound as if she had just risen from sleep, calling for Theseus across the deep water, her cheeks bedewed with tears." Titian brings Ovid's words to life in vivid color and dynamic form. Although she is mourning, and taken aback by the sudden appearance of the god and his entourage, Titian also manages to portray her budding interest in Bacchus's proposal: "Marry me and I will make you a star." Titian portrays the crown of stars above Ariadne's head representing her now-divine destiny to live in the heavens as a constellation. Master of Wine Jancis Robinson, one of the most brilliant stars in the universe of wine writing, says: "This is my favorite wine-related work of art. It offers a dramatic expression of the transformational power of wine and love."

Il Veronese (Paolo Caliari) (1528-1588) *Feast in the House of Levi*, Galleria della Academia, Venice   (oil on canvas)
   Originally commissioned as a Last Supper in 1573, Veronese went wild on this huge canvas and added all sorts of lively and unsanctioned images, including dogs, a cat, barbarians, dwarves, and drunken revelers. When he was hauled before the Inquisition to defend his work, he tried to compare it to Michelangelo's *Last Judgment* in the Vatican, but the Inquisitors replied that Michelangelo's work did not portray "drunkards nor dogs nor similar buffooneries." Fortunately, the Venetian Counsel restrained the Inquisition's zeal, and Veronese was able to get away with simply changing the name of the painting from *Last Supper* to *Feast at the House of Levi*. In words that are music to Bacchus's ears, he proclaimed: "Mine is no art of thought; my art is joyous and praises God in light and color."

Caravaggio (1571-1610). Bacchus Uffizi Gallery, Florence. (oil on canvas)
   Caravaggio's flushed-face, jejune Bacchus reclines as though he

had just staggered into a symposium or a high school prom. Portrayed with vine leaves and grapes in his hair, his left hand holds out a tumbler of red wine, beckoning us to partake. This cherubic teenage image of the god of wine reminds us of the humor inherent in the Bacchanalian way. Slight ripples on the surface of the wine in the glass suggest imminent tipsiness. Caravaggio adds another playful touch that was only discovered after the painting was

Caravaggio's *Bacchus*

cleaned: He places an image of himself working at the easel in the reflection on the glass carafe holding the wine.

Johannes "Jan" Vermeer (1632-1675) Vermeer's parents were innkeepers. Wine was an integral aspect of his life and work. His figures enjoy wine with poise and serenity, but his images posses a clarity so uncanny that they suggest something mysterious. Vermeer points to the transcendent in the everyday experience of wine.-*The Glass of Wine*. Staatliche Museum, Berlin, Germany. (oil on canvas)
-*The Girl with a Wine Glass*. Herzog Anton Ulrich-Museum, Brunswick, Germany (oil on canvas)

Jean-Baptiste-Simeon Chardin (1699-1779) Chardin's paintings celebrate the role of wine in joie de vivre in an understated, elegant way. Like Vermeer, he guides us to see the beauty that is right in front of our eyes at every meal. Especially notable among his many exceptional works are:
- *Pears, Walnuts, and a Glass of Wine*, Louvre, Paris, France (oil on canvas)
- *The Left-Overs of a Lunch*, also called *The Silver Goblet*, Musée

des Beaux-Arts, Lille, France (oil on canvas)
-*Carafe of Wine, Silver Goblet, Five Cherries, Two Peaches, an Apricot, and a Green Apple,* The Saint Louis Art Museum, St. Louis, Mo. (oil on canvas)

Frans Hals (1581-1666) A delightful counterpoint to Chardin and Vermeer, Hals's figures are lush and earthy as they drink to our health and joy.
– *Lute Player with Wine Glass,* Mansion House, London (oil on canvas)
– *The Jolly Drinker,* Rijksmuseum, Netherlands (oil on canvas)

Frans Hals:
Lute player with wine glass

Nicolas Poussin (1594–1665) Poussin was the supreme French painter of the seventeenth century. He was strongly influenced by the works of Caravaggio, Caracci, and Raphael, and he became a profound influence on generations of artists to follow including Jacques-Louis David, Paul Cezanne, and Pablo Picasso. Poussin also inspires Natalie MacLean, author of *Red, White, and Drunk All Over* whose favorite wine-related painting is:
-*The Nurture of Bacchus.* Musée du Louvre, Paris, France (oil on canvas)

A bit of background is helpful in understanding this masterpiece. Bacchus, aka Dionysus, had a rather difficult birth. Zeus, the king of the gods, impregnated his mother, the mortal woman Semele. Everything was going swimmingly until she was incinerated instantaneously after insisting, with the encouragement of Hera, the disguised and insanely jealous wife of Zeus, on gazing directly upon his countenance. Fortunately, her ivy-wrapped womb survived. Zeus plucked out the embryonic god of wine and sliced his own thigh to create a womb-like alternative for the gestation of his son. After emerging from his father's thigh as a charismatic infant god, the jealous Titans tore him to pieces and boiled his remains. But Dionysus had some hardy DNA, and when a drop of his blood fell to earth it morphed into a pomegranate tree. Zeus's mom Rhea, arranged for the fruit of the tree to be transformed into the third birth of her grandson.

Nymphs and Satyrs loved the young god of wine and ecstasy and devoted themselves to nurturing him. Since his jealous stepmother, Hera, had put out a contract on his life, Zeus arranged for Hermes to temporarily change the young god into a goat. In this magnificent painting, the baby god is refreshed by a large tumbler of wine as his alter-ego, the goat, stands by. Poussin brings to life the forces that nurture the spirit of fertility, joy and wine.

Also see: *Midas and Bacchus*, Alte Pinakothek, Munich, Germany (oil on canvas)

Wine: The Medium Is the Message

In the year 2000, Philippe Dufrenoy experienced a life-changing artistic epiphany. After losing his engineering job, the fifty-three year-old was consoling himself with a glass of red wine in a Bordeaux café. On a whim, he picked up a brush that happened to be sitting on a table nearby and dipped it into his glass. He began painting on the paper table covering and discovered his true calling: wine-inspired art painted with wine. Dufrenoy's vintage works include portraits of great chefs such as Charlie Trotter and Thomas Keller, leading wine producers like Anthony Barton from Château Leoville Barton, Alfred

Tesseron from Château Figeac, and Mike Grgich of Grgich Hills—all painted, of course, with their own wines—and a magnificent likeness of cellist Mstislav Rostropovich.

Jean Francois De Troy (1679-1752), *The Oyster Lunch*, Musee Conde, Chantilly, France (oil on canvas)

Although the name of this painting is *The Oyster Lunch*, a more apt title might be *The Champagne Launch*. De Troy's masterpiece was commissioned by King Louis XV to decorate his dining room at Versailles. It is the first depiction of a new wine that was creating a sensation in the courts of Europe: sparkling Champagne! Prior to this time the wines of the Champagne region—including those made by the legendary Benedictine monk Dom Perignon— were still, and predominantly red. The effervescent spirit of the Age of Enlightenment finds delicious expression in this painting, which captures the moment the cork flies out of the bottle.

Dom Perignon: Myth and Reality

Contemporary standards for making fine wine were pioneered by Dom Perignon (1638-1715), the cellarmaster and chief winemaker for the abbey at Hautvillers in Epernay, France. The legendary Benedictine monk wasn't blind (although he is credited with originating "blind-tasting"), he didn't invent sparkling champagne (although one of the world's great champagnes bears his name, he spent considerable effort figuring out how to *prevent* the formation of bubbles in wine, as they were considered a flaw at the time), and he didn't say " Come quickly, I'm tasting stars" (this was advertising copy for bubbly, written approximately two centuries after his death). But as Don and Petie Kladstrup explain in their masterful book

Champagne: How the World's Most Glamorous Wine Triumphed Over War and Hard Times, Dom Perignon's innovations paved the way for the evolution of the fine wines we enjoy today. He pioneered the following practices:
• Prune the vines religiousy.
• Select only the finest grapes from the harvest.
• Pick the grapes in the cool of the early morning.
• Press the grapes gently.
• Vinify the juice of each pressing separately.
• Renounce additives and unnatural processes.
• Blend the separate pressings to create something greater than the sum of its parts.

John Singer Sargent (1856 –1925) La Verre de Porto (Lit.- The Glass of Port) this painting is also known as "A Dinner Table at Night." Fine Arts Museums of San Francisco: The de Young Museum. (Oil on canvas)

An American born in Florence, Sargent spent much of his adult life based in England hobnobbing with the socialites and wealthy clients who commissioned his works.

In this painting he creates an intimate, alluring but enigmatic portrait of an elegant woman sitting at a dinner table with a man who we view in profile. He looks at her while she gazes in the direction of the decanter of red wine on the table to her right. (Wine geeks argue that despite the title of the painting, the decanter is probably filled with Claret rather than Port, as Claret was, at the time, considered the more notable symbol of good taste) Sargent fills the room with beautiful shades of crimson and claret and hints that perhaps the two subjects might loosen up and improve their communication if they drained the decanter.

Pablo Picasso (1881-1973) *Homage to Bacchus*

Picasso loved wine! *'Drink to me, drink to my health, you know I can't drink anymore.'* Those were Picasso's last words, uttered as he died on April 8, 1973 while hosting a dinner party for his friends.

Of his many wine-related works of art the greatest is probably the lithograph on display at the Museum of Wine and Culture in Rioja, Spain. Completed in 1960, it is vintage Picasso. Picasso also created the label for the 1973 vintage of Mouton Rothschild commemorating the year in which Chateau's wine was elevated to first-growth status.

The Wine Labels of Château Mouton Rothschild

Wine is art you can drink, and the art that you can't drink has become a delightful feature of the labels of many producers around the world. California's Clos Pegase Winery labels each of their bottles with a reproduction of one of their extensive collection of contemporary masterpieces, and the Hallingstad Vineyard from Norway places an image from the expressionist pioneer Edvard Munch (1863-1944) on each vintage of its Pinot Noir. Many wineries commission artists to design their labels. Among the most notable are those of Vietti, Benziger Imagery, Galante Vineyards, Montes, Justin, Red Car Wines, and Leeuwinn Estates. But the originator of this idea remains unsurpassed.

The story begins in 1924 when Baron Philippe de Rothschild (1902-1988) decided to revolutionize the world of Bordeaux by bottling his own wine. Prior to this, all the wine produced in the area was sold in barrels to agents in Bordeaux. These *negociants* then proceeded to take charge of the process of bottling, labeling, aging, and selling the wine.

When the Baron decided to make the first Medoc wine to be labeled *Mis en Bouteille au Château* (estate bottled), he effectively proclaimed that his label was a guarantee of authenticity and quality. He celebrated this innovative leap by engaging the poster artist Jean Carlu to create the Cubist-style label for the 1924 vintage.

After a number of labeling experiments and the interruption of the Second World War, the Baron, beginning in 1946, commissioned an original work of art for each vintage.

He asked each artist to express the themes of the joy of wine, the beauty of the vines and the vineyards, and/or the image of his chateau's symbol—the ram. (The French word mouton is similar to mutton in English, and translates as "sheep" or "ram".) Among the most notable examples:

1947: Jean Cocteau	1974: Robert Motherwell
1955: Georges Braque	1975: Andy Warhol
1958: Salvador Dalí	1982: John Huston
1969: Joan Miró	1983: Saul Steinberg
1970: Marc Chagall	1988: Keith Haring
1971: Wassily Kandinsky	2004: Prince Charles
1973: Pablo Picasso	

We can gain a further appreciation into the role of wine as an inspiration for art by recognizing that all these renowned artists happily accepted cases of Mouton in lieu of cash payment.

> *"I love the labels of Mouton-Rothschild, especially Marc Chagall's for the 1970 vintage. But I think the greatest wine-related art is the landscape architecture of the world's great wine regions. There's nothing more beautiful than the vineyards themselves."*
> —Kevin Zraly on his favorite wine-related work of art

Temples of Wine

The first great wine-inspired architecture was the Temple of Dionysus on the eastern slope of the Acropolis in Athens. Although an increasing number of fine wines are made in garages and in generic, high-tech blending facilities, a number of wineries around the world have created architectural masterpieces. Among the greatest contemporary Dionysian temples are:

Marqués de Riscal - Designed by Frank Gehry, the Pritzker Prize-winning architect, this winery in Rioja, Spain, bears a striking resemblance to Gehry's Guggenheim Museum in Bilbao.

Bodegas Ysios - Another magnificent winery in the Rioja region, this estate is fully integrated into the landscape, at the foot of the Sierra de Cantabria mountains. The architect Santiago Calatrava was inspired by the image of an outline of a row of wine barrels.

Bodega Septima - Designed by architects Eliana Bórmida and Mario Yanzón. This Argentinean winery was constructed with a building technique used for centuries by the native tribes of the region based on cutting and piling up natural stones from the Andes mountain range.

Chateau Pichon-Longueville - There are many exquisite chateaux in Bordeaux, including Lynch-Bages and Latour but Pichon-Longueville is perhaps the finest example of a magical castle of wine.

The Robert Mondavi Winery - Designed by Cliff May, in Oakville California, the Mondavi Winery is the architectural manifestation of Mondavi's vision to bring the culture of wine to America. Across the street, at Opus One, he collaborated with the Rothschilds to create a post-modern winery that seems to have been beamed down from the Starship Enterprise.

The Dominus Estate - Another Napa Valley masterpiece,

designed by the Pritzker Prize-winning team of Jacques Herzog and Pierre de Meuron (designers of the Tate Modern in London). Locals have nicknamed it the "stealth winery" because it blends effortlessly into the surrounding landscape. As Christian Moueix of Dominus explains, the architectural statement, "echoes our belief that the vineyard is of utmost importance."

Turnbull Wine Cellars - The Johnson Turnbull Wine Vineyards was founded by the award winning architect William Turnbull in 1979. He designed it to be low key and in tune with its environment. He explains, "You want to have an image of a winery that cares about the last drop of wine in the bottle."(In the spring of 1993, Patrick O'Dell purchased the winery and renamed it Turnbull Wine Cellars.)

Sterling Vineyards - Sterling's striking Mediterranean-style design was inspired by the brilliant white stucco buildings on the Greek island of Mykonos. Nestled three hundred feet above the town of Calistoga in between the Mayacamas and Vaca mountains, Sterling's aerial tram offers thrilling views of Napa Valley.

The Clos Pegase Winery - Jan Shrem, the founder of Clos Pegase, made his millions in publishing. He jokes, "the best way to make a small fortune in Napa Valley is to start with a large one." Working with the assistance of the San Francisco Museum of Modern Art, Shrem selected architect Michael Graves to design a "temple to wine and art" in California's premiere wine district. Completed in 1987, the winery includes a magnificent sculpture garden and a permanent exhibition of some of the world's greatest twentieth-century art. Shrem emphasizes that it's "not a museum or a sacred shrine way up in the clouds, but a haven here on earth. The kind of place we know Bacchus would approve of, where art and vines seem to spring from the same fertile soil, where smiling is encouraged, and pleasure and serendipity are all around you."

Now eighty years old, Shrem travels the world inspiring people about his wines. He explains the confluence of his love of art, architecture, and wine: "In architecture, as in our wines, I believe we have achieved balance, harmony, and symmetry in the classical Greek sense, avoiding the baroque concepts of high oak, high alcohol, and high extract to create food-friendly wines of quiet elegance."

The winery name springs from the French word for an enclosed vineyard—*clos*—and Pegase, French for Pegasus, the winged steed who unleashed the spring of the muses. Shrem's favorite painting in his collection of more than one thousand masterpieces is by the great nineteenth century French artist Odilon Redon (1840-1916): Redon depicts Pegasus with his front hooves raising up toward the heavens, his back hooves planted firmly on the earth. Another special treasure in the collection is Henry Moore's sculpture "Gaia." In Greek mythology Gaia is the source of all living things, including the vine and its fruit. Shrem also delights in a carved figure of a naked man holding a goblet and decanter. This is Ganymede, the sommelier for the gods on Mount Olympus. As Shrem says, "His job was to pour the wine, as is ours."

Other wineries notable for their art or architecture include the Hess Collection, Artesa, Cade, Darioush, Del Dotto and Domaine Carneros (California), the Peregrine winery (New Zealand), I. Boutaris & Son (Santorini, Greece), the Perez Cruz winery (Maipo Valley, Chile), Vergelegen Wine Estate (Stellenbosch, South Africa), Domaine Disznoko (Tokaj, Hungary), Alois Lageder Vineyards (Alto Adige, Italy) and the Leo Hillinger winery (Austria).

Wine Is the Muse

"Music is the wine that fills the cup of silence"
— Robert Fripp, King Crimson guitarist

In the first installment of his autobiography, entitled *My Young Years*, the magnificent virtuoso pianist Arthur Rubinstein (1887-1982) recounts a delightful story about his favorite composer, Johannes Brahms (1833-1897). Brahms was being entertained by a renowned wine connoisseur who hoped to impress his special guest. The host filled the maestro's glass as he proclaimed, "This is the Brahms of my cellar!" Brahms swirled, sniffed, sipped, and then sat silently. The host inquired anxiously, "Is it to your liking?" Brahms replied, "Hmmm, better bring me your Beethoven."

Like Brahms, Beethoven loved and was inspired by wine. In *The Life of Ludwig Van Beethoven,* biographer Alexander Thayer notes, "Beethoven was accustomed to drinking wine from youth up." Beethoven apparently had a great capacity for drinking without displaying the effects— "he drank a great deal at table, but he could stand a great deal." Thayer mentions, however, that when inspired by the conviviality of his friends he could sometimes get a bit "tipsy."

Beethoven wrote, "Music is the wine which inspires one to new generative processes, and I am Bacchus who presses out this glorious wine for mankind and makes them spiritually drunken."

As Beethoven proclaims, music and wine go hand in hand when it comes to inspiring creativity. The worlds of jazz, rock, and blues feature many wonderful wine-inspired compositions, such as Grover Washington Jr.'s "Winelight" and the Moody Blues' "Vintage Wine," and the great Bluesman Buddy Guy sings of his yearning to return to the south where "the water tastes like cherry wine."

But for the ultimate tribute to the grape we turn to the world of opera.

It's hard to imagine opera without wine. If there was no Café Momus, there would be no *La Boheme*. If Falstaff didn't have his sherry and hot wine for fortification… well, he wouldn't be Falstaff. The Italian composer Gioachino Antonio Rossini (1792 –1868) wrote thirty-nine operas including *The Barber of Seville, Cinderella*, and *William Tell*. Rossini's love of wine began in childhood with his first taste at mass. His wine cellar held the best of Bordeaux and a phenomenal collection of Port sent by one of his biggest fans, the King of Portugal. Rossini was a renowned gastronome and inspired a number of famous dishes, including turkey stuffed with black truffles (Turkey Rossini) and filet mignon with foie gras and truffles (Tournedos Rossini). He especially loved dessert wines and referred to them as expressions of "angelic harmony."

Rossini is one of the composers featured in the wonderful book *Opera & Wine: Wine in Opera* by Valentino Monticello. Monticello explores the confluence of wine, opera and art through a unique medium: wine labels. He notes, "All of my pictures are composed of shapes carefully cut from wine labels; the people, the flowers, even the lines, are all cut from different wine labels. There is no drawing or painting involved at all."

A former Head Sommelier at Harry's Bar in London, Monticello is also a lifelong devotee of opera. With the help of his colleague Luciano Citeroni, he researched opera libretti to discover wine-related themes. He discovered seventy-four and he then created an original work of art, using wine labels, to pay homage to the countries where the opera was set, written, or first performed. He provides a thoughtful guide to the wines and winegrowing regions referenced in each opera. Monticello's work has been featured at the Summer Exhibition at the Royal Academy of Art and at Christie's auction house in London. His remarkable series *The Life of Bacchus* is on exhibition at the acclaimed Il Molino di Grace (www.ilmolinodigrace.com) vineyard in Tuscany.

The Birth of Opera: Pleasure Beyond Belief

Although there are many precursors, music historians generally agree that the first opera was performed in Florence in 1598. Composed by tenor Jacopo Peri (1561-1633), with a libretto by the poet Ottavio Rinuccini (1562-1621), the subject was Ovid's story of Apollo and Daphne. According to Rinuccini, this first opera "gave pleasure beyond belief to the few who heard it." Peri and Rinuccini were students of a group of scholars known as the Florentine Camerata, a group that included Vincenzo Galilei (1520-1591), Galileo's father. The Camerata convened a few times a month at the palace of Count Giovanni di' Bardi (1534-1612) to share wine, philosophy, and poetry as they explored classical Greek drama and music. The Camerata felt that the ancient Greek performances at the Temple of Dionysus held profound secrets to stirring the soul. Their exploration of these secrets set the stage for the work of Claudio Monteverdi (1567-1643) the father of modern opera. Monteverdi conceived of the orchestra as we know it today, and he composed at least eighteen operas. In his glorious madrigal *Venite, venite*, Monteverdi compares God's grace to an unlimited supply of free food and wine.

Although he abstained on performance days, Luciano Pavarotti (1935-2007) fortified his incomparable tenor voice with his favorite wines, Gavi di Gavi and Lambrusco di Sorbara. Dame Kiri Te Kanawa (1944—), the great soprano, told a reporter from London's *Telegraph* newspaper, "Food and wine fascinate me. They bring people together, are ice-breakers between strangers and teach one so much about a place." A former vineyard owner, the Kiwi coloratura prefers the Sauvignon Blancs and Pinot Noirs of her native New Zealand. She confesses to a passion for great champagne, including favorites such as Dom

Perignon, Cristal, and La Grande Dame. She comments, "It doesn't matter how often I have a glass, I just lap it up."

Among the great wine-related operatic songs, the following are especially notable:

• "Libiamo," Alfredo's aria from La Traviata, by Giusseppe Verdi (1813-1901)
Alfredo sings
Let us drink, for with wine
love will enjoy yet more passionate kisses.
Be happy... wine and song
and laughter beautify the night...

• "Drinking Song" from *Hamlet* by Ambrogio Thomas (1811-1896)
The famous drinking song begins,
"O wine, dispel the sorrow that weighs heavily on my heart."

• "Viva il vino spumaggiante" from *Cavalleria Rusticana* by Pietro Mascagni (1863-1945) and "Toast to King Champagne" from *Die Fledermaus* by Johann Strauss II (1825–1899)

Bubbly is especially beloved in the opera world. In Mascagni's Cavalleria Rusticana, Turiddu sings *viva il vino spumaggiante,* "here's to the sparkling wine," and *Die Fledermaus* by Johann Strauss features one of opera's greatest drinking songs, the "Toast to King Champagne." The main character of this Strauss operetta isn't Eisenstein, Rosalinde, Falke, or Orlovsky—it's Champagne!

This excerpt from *Fledermaus* captures the flavor of effervescent celebration:
Eisenstein: "A toast to the life of our party, - to King Champagne!"
Orlovsky: "Champagne's delicious bubbles, tra la la la la la la la

Scatter all our troubles, tra la la la la la la la
It mellows politicians and betters world conditions.
All diplomats and rulers
Should keep it in the coolers.
We toast Champagne, the essence of the essence,
The King of Effervescence!"

• The opening scene of *The Elixir of Love,* by Gaetano
Donizetti (1797-1848)

Champagne is to *Die Fledermaus* as Claret is to Gaetano
Donizetti's *L'elisir d'amore* (The Elixir of Love/The Love Potion). In
the opening scene, the itinerant quack Dr. Dulcamara sells the love-sick
peasant Nemorino a magic potion guaranteed to help him win the heart
of the lovely Adina. In an aside to the audience the doctor admits "E'
bordo, non elisir!" (It's not an elixir, it's Bordeaux!)

Master of Wine Jancis Robinson's favorite wine-related music is another piece by Donizetti: *Lucrezia Borgia.* Robinson notes that although
it doesn't end happily, Act II, Scene 3 begins in joyous praise of wine.
First, with a toast to Madeira then to the wine of the Rhine and another
to the nectar of Cyprus.

Then Orsini sings:

"I praise the cup whose flowing
With golden glorious glowing
Wakes Cupid from his trance
In thy seducing glance"

• Falstaff's aria from Falstaff by Giuseppe Verdi (1813-1901)

Valentino Monticello describes this song as: "One of Verdi's most
expressive compositions where the musical tonality captures the
mood of a sad deceitful world and the almost dreamlike joy that one
can find in a glass of wine."

Music: Wine Is the Medium

Just as Phillippe Dufrenoy finds his muse through wine-in-spired paintings done with wine, Australian musician Tony King creates music using a variety of wine-related objects, including bottles, glasses, barrels, corks, and wine itself. What does it sound like? Imagine a meditative, jazzy cross between the pan flute of Zamfir and Balinese gamelan music. You can hear a sample at: www.soundofwine.net

Opening Our Hearts, Freeing Our Minds

*"A full cup of wine at the right time
is worth more than all the kingdoms of this earth!"*
—Gustav Mahler (1860-1911)
from *Das Lied Von Der Erde* (The Song of the Earth)

To paraphrase Beethoven, "Wine is the muse that inspires one to new generative processes." Trombonist Abbie Conant, the first woman to hold a principal chair in a major German orchestra, finds wine to be such a muse. The story of Conant's success in the face of discrimination based on her gender has been featured in the *Wall Street Journal*, on National Public Radio, and in Malcolm Gladwell's best-seller *Blink*. Conant comments on the connection between wine and music: "Like fine wine, great music leaves a 'positive hangover' of good feelings, renewed hope, revitalized imagination, and inspiration. Fine wine and beautiful music can both serve to sensitize us and help us open our hearts and free our minds. Or drinking can dull our senses, and we can listen to music that pounds us into banality and lethargy. We make the choice and cultivate our 'taste' accordingly."

"When I sip a superior wine (one that makes my socks go up and down) I sense the poetic spirit of humankind embodied in the rarified juice of grapes. The alchemy of winemaking turns simple grapes into something transcendent, a liquid essence of the spirit of culture, earth, and sun. In making music we become the vessel out of which pours the human song—we devote ourselves to making the transcendent audible. Great wine and great music celebrate our ability to use our senses to exalt our spirits—bringing earth and heaven together."

Music: Vino Paradiso

Carlo Cignozzi of *Paradiso di Frassina* winery near Montalcino in Tuscany plays the music of Mozart, Handel and Vivaldi over loudspeakers to serenade the Sangiovese grapes in his vineyard. Cignozzi says that his fruit becomes more robust and flavorful when exposed to classical music around the clock. Researchers from Florence University are studying his methods and Professor of Agriculture Stefano Mancuso notes that although the results aren't yet conclusive it appears that the music has "positive effects on vine growth."
www.alparadisodifrassina.it

Wine drinking has inspired creative thinking throughout human history. Wine played a central role in the culture of the ancient Egyptians and Chinese. For the Greeks, who gave us much of the basis of our language and culture, wine was the catalyst for the Symposium, where philosophy was born. The divine juice of the grape has always played a significant role in the rituals and sacraments of the Judeo-Christian tradition. Prized by the Romans, wine was also the liquid muse for many Renaissance masters. For Thomas Jefferson and the other Founding Fathers, it was a necessity of life. Wine has been both the catalyst and the subject of great art, architecture, and music through the ages.

[PART 3]

THE NEW SYMPOSIUM

"What interests me is the effect on the
emotions, the happy state of mind that wine
causes even before it is drunk. The prospect of
wine is so pleasant that it relaxes the face
muscles and makes one's eyes light up.
Even before the cork is drawn, a good bottle
induces a festive atmosphere of good humor
and relaxation."
—Emile Peynaud (1912-2004),
pioneering oenologist and author of
The Taste of Wine: The Art and Science

How to Do the Wine Drinking for Inspired Thinking Exercise

"From wine what sudden friendship springs!"
—John Gay (1685 – 1732),
English poet and dramatist

I love to bring people together. And I love to inspire creative thinking. I do it for a living but it's also as an integral part of my life. My wife and I enjoy wine on a regular basis and we share our experience in poetic terms a few times every week. Once a month or so, we invite friends to our home for a New Symposium, a salon organized around a comparative wine-tasting.

The experience of wine-inspired, poetic conviviality translates into a very effective means for bringing all kinds of groups together. Bringing people together in a creative way is especially important in the organizational world. Patrick Lencioni, author of the best-selling leadership fable *The Five Dysfunctions of a Team*, emphasizes, "Not finance. Not strategy. Not technology. It is teamwork that remains the ultimate competitive advantage, both because it is so powerful and so rare." Lencioni argues that absence of trust predicated on a lack of openness, a reluctance to share vulnerabilities, and avoidance of communication about mistakes combine to provide the primary obstacles to *esprit d'corps*. Before teams can align around a common purpose they must develop the ability to embrace conflict and engage in passionate, constructive debate. This is just what the ancient Greek Symposium was designed to accomplish.

When asked by *Management Consulting News* to give just one piece of advice to a new team leader, Lencioni responded, "Take the risk of being vulnerable with the people you lead. That means be open about who you are, what your concerns are, what your strengths and weaknesses are. Be human, and they will trust you." The Wine Drinking for Inspired Thinking exercise that you are about to learn is a simple, disarming, humanizing process that promotes the openness and trust that contribute to team success. It also inspires deeper bonding and a shared experience of *la dolce vita* amongst friends and family groups.

Bacchus in the Boardroom

The number one request my clients make is: "Please help us think out-of-the-box."

The next most common request is: "Please help us with team building."

When clients ask for help with team building, it's a good idea to begin by asking them what kind of activities they've tried in the past. You might be surprised at how often team-building exercises go awry:

• An engineer from a chemical firm explained that his group was sent on a "High ropes course." As he told it, "One of the guys fell off and broke his arm. Yes, there was something about riding in the ambulance on the way to the hospital that really helped bring our team together."

• An investment manager from a major pension fund shared the story of her group's white-water rafting adventure: "One of the women fell overboard and drowned. I was impressed with the power of a funeral to bring our group closer."

The examples above are somewhat exaggerated for your amusement, but the following story of a team-building event with unintended consequences is true. As reported in the *New York Times* on October 8, 2001:

"WORKERS BOND, THEN ARE TREATED"

The article described an event held in Florida featuring an exercise that required participants to walk on hot coals. The result, according to

the *Times:* "About a dozen ... marketing department workers burned their feet last week when they walked over white-hot coals at a meeting intended to promote bonding. One woman spent a day in a hospital...a doctor [was called] to treat others whose feet were blistered. Some workers used wheelchairs when they went to the airport to leave for another company retreat."

Believe it or not, they were all employees of a national hamburger chain known for their "flame-broiled" product.

The philosophy behind a lot of team-building seems to be something like this:

You've been complaining that your job is very stressful. So we are going to take you out of your very stressful job for a day or two and make you do something even more stressful so that when we send you back to work you will stop complaining.

The Wine Drinking for Inspired Thinking exercise is based on a different philosophy of bringing people together: **Create a relaxed and enjoyable atmosphere and then gently guide participants to get a glimpse of the creative spark in their colleagues and themselves.**

In the sometimes-soulless world of commerce we need to create an environment where the soul can shine, where we can gain insight and appreciation of the hidden depths of our associates and ourselves. The key is to do this without causing any unnecessary additional stress and to avoid invasive, touchy-feely encounter-group activities.

Fine wine and poetry are the perfect catalysts.

Whether you aim to bring a team together at work or to facilitate greater *joie de vivre* with your friends and guests, the process is basically the same, and delightfully simple.

The exercise has five phases:

1-Set the Stage

2-Give an Overview

3-Taste the Wine
4-Write Poetry
5-Read and Celebrate

1.Set the Stage

"The only pain should be Champagne."
—Team-building motto

When I was growing up, my parents' house was the center of the neighborhood. Other children came over all the time, probably because my mom always had lots of good food available. Our Jewish-Italian heritage made food and hospitality a prominent part of everyday life.

This tradition continues at our home today. When we aren't on the road, my wife and I shop for fresh food daily, and we cook for our friends every week. And we love to host wine and poetry evenings. Organizing this event at home is easy. All you need to do is get some good wine glasses, choose the wine, and have some paper and pens available. Once we've chosen the wines we will go online and look up the website of the producers. It's easy to download, print, and copy fact sheets about most wines. We hand these out to our guests to answer all their "left-brain" questions about the wine.

If you are holding this event for colleagues or clients at a hotel or restaurant, then a bit more planning is necessary. I've conducted this event in a Palm Springs hotel ballroom for four hundred training managers and at the Venetian Hotel in Las Vegas for a group of forty company presidents. And in the real Venice and at Disneyworld, and at retreat centers, restaurants, and wineries all over the world. The ideal venue, if you aren't at home, is a place with a great wine list, superb food, service and ambiance.

Once you've chosen a venue, consider the staff supporting your event and elements such as timing, glassware and, of course, the wine.

Brief the serving staff and recruit them to support the spirit of the event. If there's an in-house sommelier, then by all means ask him to help in the wine selection. You can also invite the sommelier to give a brief talk to the group about the wine, focusing on where and how it was made, the history of the vineyards, the nature of the vintages, etc.

Place sticky colored dots, ribbons, or washable marker symbols on the base of the wine glasses so people can discern the different wines after they are poured. (Experience shows that attempting to remember the order of the wines by pouring, for example, from left to right, is a noble but usually unsuccessful strategy.) Remember to place a pad of paper and a pen at each person's table setting, for note-taking and po-etry writing.

Plan to begin the tasting before dinner so that people can bring their full attention to the wine. At a recent event for software executives in the Northwest we began by comparing two sparkling wines: the 1997 Argyle Extended Tirage Brut from Oregon and the Duval-Leroy NV Brut from France. The wines were poured into flutes on separate tables and participants were invited to help themselves.

After the bubbly, the group was invited to sit at the dinner tables and explore the three glasses of Syrah that awaited them: the Penfold's St. Henri Shiraz 2002 from Australia, The Cayuse Syrah Walla Walla Valley Bionic Frog 2002 from Washington, and The Ojai Syrah 2002 Roll Ranch Ventura from California.

These particular wines were chosen because they made the neatest comparison (same year and grape from different regions) and because they all happened to be delicious and available on the wine list at not unreasonable prices.

The event also featured a comparative tasting of fine chocolates from different regions, both to enhance the pleasure and to offer a spe-cial focus for the two members of the group who didn't drink wine.

In summary, carefully think through the venue, the order of the events, and be sure to align all logistics (pens, pads, glasses, coordina-tion of servers and staff, timing, etc). If people aren't staying over at the venue then it's essential to arrange transportation so that no one has to drive afterward.

2- Give an Overview

"In water one sees one's own face; but in wine,
one beholds the heart of another."
—French proverb

Before any wine is served, give an overview of the exercise. Let your guests know how the event will unfold and reassure everyone that it will be fun. Anticipate the most common concerns and address them. For example, most people don't think of themselves as "poetic." At a recent event someone exclaimed:

"This will never work. We're not poets."

You can expect some version of this objection almost every time you lead this exercise. You can reassure everyone by pointing out that, "After the second glass of wine, everyone is a poet."

"But what about the people in our group who don't drink?"

No problem. Ask them to share poetic observations about some aspect of their experience. You may wish to include a comparative tasting of fine chocolates and to play some great music. You can also offer a comparative tasting of fine Chinese teas. The non-drinkers don't miss a beat. (At a recent event a gentleman whose religious background had precluded him from ever tasting wine was one of the poetry contest winners. His poem, which caused a number of women in the audience to swoon, began, "Oh ruby red goddess, I will never kiss your lips.")

Another common obstacle to a successful event is that some people suspect wine is too fancy; they associate it with pretension and inaccessible rituals. Underlying those concerns is the general challenge to adult learning — the fear of embarrassment.

In a program for a group of business analysts one gentleman expressed his discomfort by asking a question about a comparison between the Sauvignon Blancs from Cloudy Bay (New Zealand) and Caymus (California). In a voice loud enough for everyone to hear, he demanded, "Which of these goes better with Bud Light?" Without hesitation I suggested the Cloudy Bay would complement the Bud Light and that the Caymus is best with Miller Genuine Draft.

Humor is useful to help defuse anxiety about making mistakes. Remember not to take the process, or yourself, too seriously.

Frame the exercise in the context of creative exploration, right-hemisphere appreciation, fun, and enjoyment. Let people know that there will be wonderful prizes for the most evocative poetry. (Bottles of the best wines or boxes of chocolate are always well received.)

In the introduction you'll also want to help your group understand the difference between left-hemisphere analysis and right-hemisphere, multi-sensory appreciation. As your group realizes that there will be no wrong answers, they relax and open to a new experience of creative enjoyment and fun.

3 - Taste the Wine

Caveat! Use the very highest quality wine that you can obtain. It's better to have less wine of greater quality rather than more wine of lesser quality. Ideally, you will have more wine of greater quality. The key point is that below a certain qualitative level you will not inspire poetry. You will only get limericks, such as "I once had some wine in a bucket..."

Once you've set the stage and offered a brief introduction and overview it can be helpful, and fun, to guide everyone through the Sensazione-7 approach to tasting and enjoying wine. Let's review:

1-See: Bring people's attention to the color and clarity of the wine
2-Swirl: Ask everyone to stand and practice swirling their wine. Encourage them to try the "hula-hoop" swirl.
3-Smell: Demonstrate plunging your nose into the glass and in-

haling dramatically. Ask everyone to follow.

4-Sip/Slurp: Demonstrate sipping, while making loud slurping noises. This helps everyone avoid taking themselves or the process too seriously.

5-Swallow/Spit: Encourage your group to be aware of the texture, weight, and flavors as they swallow. You might also suggest that they practice exhaling through the nose while swallowing. This heightens the sensations and also inspires laughter when someone inadvertently reverse snorts wine through their nose.

6-Savor: Remind your group to pause after swallowing, with eyes closed, so they can notice and enjoy the continuing sensations, flavors, and nuances of the wine.

7-Share: Reinforce the notion that there are no wrong answers to the question: How do you experience this wine? Encourage the expression of analogical musings to set the stage for the next step of the New Symposium.

4 - Write Poetry

If with water you fill up your glasses,
You'll never write anything wise
But wine is the horse of Parnassus
That carries a bard to the skies.
—Athenaeus (second century A.D.)
in *The Deipnosophistae (The Learned Banqueters)*

Now, ask every one to express their experience of the wine in poetic terms.

You can make it easier for people to begin by trying these simple exercises:

• Ask people to write down the first five words they think of after tasting the wine. Then suggest that they use those words to begin crafting a poem.

• Read these questions aloud (as introduced in Part 1), to help people get in the mood to think analogically. Divide people into small groups of three or four and ask them to share their responses. This always yields lively dialogue and stimulates everyone's poetic imagination.

-If this wine were a style of music, what would it be?

-If this wine were a painting, who would be the artist?

-If this wine had a shape, what would it be?

-If this wine could dance, what dance would it do?

-If this wine were a car, what would it be?

-If this wine were a kiss from a celebrity, who would it be?

-If this wine were an item of clothing, what might it be?

• It can also be helpful to give each person a pad of blank paper and colored pens and suggest that they "creatively doodle" the colors and shapes associated with their experience of each wine. As they draw the aromas, textures, and taste of the wines, poetic language emerges spontaneously.

Why express the experience of the wine in poetic language? There are many wonderful reasons.

Once you create an environment in which people feel safe from ridicule and embarrassment, the invitation to poetry awakens the creative part of the mind. This more analogical and metaphorical mode taps people into their intuition and facilitates an ambiance of openness and playful exploration. This ambiance makes it much easier to bond with others; and the poetic descriptions enhance the experience of appreciating the wine, making it more memorable and pleasurable.

David Whyte, author of *The Heart Aroused: Poetry and the Preservation of the Soul in Corporate America,* is a pioneer in helping individuals and organizations liberate their muses and allow their creative juices to flow. Whyte explains the importance of poetic awareness to help us work more creatively: "Organizations need to understand the wellsprings of human creativity in order to shape conversations that are invitational to an individual's greater powers. Poetry can provide explosive insight, grant needed courage and stir the dormant imagination of individuals and organizations alike."

He adds, "A poem can often articulate something that you've only intuited, but haven't been able to say.... poetry is an incredible lifeline to anyone who's looking for a community of understanding. Poetry helps to place you into a larger context. It can help you overcome parts of you that are static... that you yourself are fed up with. It can also help to 'emancipate' you into the next phase of your existence."

Music: In-synch with what you drink

You can further enrich the experience of your Wine Drinking for Inspired Thinking event by playing music to accompany the festivities. Listening to music can significantly improve the experience of wine enjoyment. Researchers at Edinburgh's Heriot-Watt University discovered that "playing a certain type of music can enhance the way wine tastes." Subjects reported that, when accompanied by the right music, the experience of enjoyment was up to 60 percent greater. The research was sponsored by Aurelio Montes, the pioneering Chilean winemaker.

Montes is a music lover who plays Gregorian chants in his cellars to serenade his finest wines as they mature.

Professor Adrian North and his team discovered that the enjoyment of Cabernet Sauvignon was most affected by "powerful and heavy" music like Carl Orff's *Carmina Burana*, while Merlot was best accompanied by "mellow and soft" sounds like Otis Redding's "Sitting on the dock of the bay" or The Commodore's "Easy." North suggests, "Wine manufacturers could recommend that while drinking a certain wine, you should listen to a certain sort of music."

Wine-lover Don Campbell is the author of the best-seller *The Mozart Effect*. His research has demonstrated the benefits of well-chosen music in improving memory, awareness, creativity, and learning ability. He's also led the effort to demonstrate the positive effects of music in overcoming depression, anxiety, and a number of learning disabilities. He comments, "Given what we know about the effects of music on the brain, it's not at all surprising that the right music will improve the experience of wine." Campbell adds, "On a personal note, I find that wine enhances my enjoyment of music and that music deepens my appreciation of wine."

5 - Read and Celebrate

"Wine reveals what is hidden."
—Erathostenes, (275-194 BC) Greek philosopher

Remind people to write legibly and to sign their poems so they can receive prizes. Collect all the poetry around the time that the main course completes. Then sort through the entries and determine the winners. Award prizes for the most evocative, life-affirming, and hilarious poems. You can read a series of Honorable Mentions first and then the grand prize-winners. Depending on the size of the group and the timing you may wish to ask people to come up and read their own poems, but there's a delightful dramatic effect that takes place when the Master of Ceremonies (known to the ancient Greeks as the Symposiarch—the "king of the symposium") reads a poem and everyone's trying to guess who wrote it. When the name of the poem's author is announced the poet invariably receives huge applause and sometimes looks of utter astonishment. Most groups are amazed and deeply moved by the beauty of their colleague's expression.

The poems usually fall into a few regular categories:

❦ Funny ❦

"A man cannot make him laugh - but that's no marvel;
he drinks no wine."
—Shakespeare, *Henry IV*

The great English poet Alexander Pope observed, "Wine can of their wits the wise beguile, make the sage frolic, and the serious smile."

Even the most serious groups are beguiled by the combination of wine and poetry. The process yields an abundance of silly, funny, and often hilarious poems. And, yes, even the finest wines can still sometimes inspire limericks. Here's a silly one from a recent event for a group of entrepreneurs in Portland, Oregon:

There once was a man named Gelb
Whose name rhymed with nothing normelb.
His talk was convincing
(about Leonardo daVinci)
And we staggered out feeling quite welb.

A wine-loving Organizational Development specialist penned these lines after enjoying a Champagne and two Australian Shirazes:

The first wine was bubbly and fizzy
It made me feel subtly dizzy
Sipped from a flute
The terroir was gout
He's not opening another one, is he?

The second wine is bright and purple
It smells good so I'll take a slurple
It goes down with aplomb
Wow, what a fruit bomb
My feelings are now beyond verbal

The next wine is richer and darker
96 points from Bob Parker
I'm feeling quite loose
From this awesome juice
I'm tasting each gluon and quark, er.

Torrential waves of laughter are the norm, and laughing is the heart of bringing people together. As author and essayist Washington Irving (1783–1859) observed, "Honest good humor is the oil and wine of a merry meeting, and there is no jovial companionship equal to that where the jokes are rather small and laughter abundant."

🍇 Romantic, Sensual and Sexy 🍇

After conducting this exercise with many different kinds of people, it's clear that the more conservative the group, the more sensual and sexy the poetry. The poetic framework allows groups a healthy way to release their repressed energy.

After a enjoying a 1997 La Renina Brunello di Montalcino, a
Ph.D. biochemist exulted:

> *Drawn by your crimson lusciousness*
> *Tantalized by your scent*
> *Enter my lips, dance over my tongue.*
> *Embracing the fullness of your body*
> *Inviting a journey of sense and soul*
> *One touch*
> *One taste*
> *This moment*
> *Sweet, warm, release.*

Three great Washington State Meritage wines inspired a software
developer to write:

> *The grape, the crushing*
> *The waiting-the longing*
> *Longing for the look.*
> *The reflection in the eyes*
> *The kiss, slow-teasing*
> *The kiss, deeper-filling, fulfilling...*
> *The Sun, Moon, Clouds, Rains, Wind, Fire –*
> *All becoming the grape*
> *The grape flowing into nectar.*
>
> *The grape, the crushing*
> *The embrace-the heightened heart*
> *The connection-the way-the moment,*
> *Now.*

And Jennifer Rosen, author of *The Cork Jester's Guide to Wine*, advises:

> *"If you can't get your date to undress, go*
> *and buy her a fine Barbaresco.*
> *Get the girl sipping*
> *and soon she'll be stripping*
> *and begging to do it alfresco."*

Wine, Beauty, and the Eye of the Beholder

A survey conducted by researchers at Scotland's Glasgow University concluded that consuming two glasses of wine improves the perceived attractiveness of a prospective romantic partner by more than 25 percent!

🍷 Cathartic 🍷

"Give me wine to wash me clean of the weather-stains of care."
—Ralph Waldo Emerson

In the appropriate setting and dosage, wine has a delightfully cathartic effect.

Hugh Johnson explains, "It was not the subtle bouquet of wine, or lingering aftertastes of violets and raspberries, that first caught the attention of our ancestors. It was, I'm afraid, its effect."

Johnson adds, "How can a rare bottle of wine fetch the price of a great work of art? Can it, however perfect, smell more beautiful than a rose? No, must surely be the honest answer. But what if, deep in the flushing velvet of its petals, the rose contained the power to banish care?"

The president of a construction management firm expresses this effect in simple, delightful terms:

Wine,
My children like to whine
But after a couple of glasses
You know,
It's really fine.

And Lord Byron reflects:
"Wine cheers the sad, revives the old, inspires the
young, makes weariness forget his toil, and fear her dan-
ger, opens a new world, when this, the present, palls."

🍷 Haiku 🍷

"Language is wine upon the lips."
—Virginia Woolf

Every group offers a sizable percentage of the Zen-inspired poetry form of haiku that most of us learned in high school. Although it's rare to get strict examples of the correct syllabic distribution (5-7-5) the haiku spirit is alive in many attempts.

Lane Steinberg is a guitarist and songwriter who loves red wine and expresses his passion for it on his Red Wine Haiku blog. He explains, "My elderly junior high school English teacher, Miss Gimpel, introduced me to haiku. I had a real fondness for her, but her enthusiasm for haiku didn't make much of an impression on me then. My earliest memory of drinking red wine is sharing a bottle of Night Train with a dishwasher at the summer camp where I worked as a waiter. I didn't like that much, either. But now, years later, it seems to me that haiku is the perfect vehicle to encapsulate all aspects of red wine, from the mysteriously sublime to the numbingly mundane." Lane suggests that when the

haikus are good, "you should be able to taste them in your mind."
He graciously agreed to share the following examples.

Pago Florentino Tinto 2004 (Spain)

A mid-section kick
Unexpected precision
Chocolate violins

Proyetco 2000 (Spain)

Starts like weird Pinot
Finishes off like good tea
Spanish cross-dresser

Rust En Vrede Estate 1999 (South Africa)

Chocolate, green peppers
Soft round breasts in a steel bra
Pick mushrooms naked

🍇 Cynical 🍇

A small minority sometimes can't help but express their still-armored feelings. Cynics are best viewed with compassion. They are usually broken-hearted idealists. In most cases, however, they grudgingly report that the exercise was worth doing and they'll even admit to enjoying themselves.

Moreover, cynics remind us, as T. G. Shaw observed in 1864, "in wine-tasting and wine-talk there is an enormous amount of humbug." Novelist Kingsley Amis (1922-1995) penned a deliciously cynical comment about wine-appreciation: "When I find someone ... writing about an edgy, nervous wine that dithered in the glass, I cringe. When I hear someone ...talking about an austere, unforgiving wine, I turn a bit austere and unforgiving myself. When I come across stuff like that and remember about the figs and bananas, I want to snigger uneasily. You can call a wine red, and dry, and strong, and pleasant. After that, watch out."

Of course, we must bear in mind that Amis was an unrepentant over-indulger who preferred Bloody Marys with tomato ketchup, Guinness mixed with gin and ginger, and red wine with lemonade.

Along with Amis, the British journalist Auberon Waugh (1939-2001) ranks as one of the most entertaining wine cynics. Waugh, who shamelessly used his position as a wine writer to attract as many free samples as possible, was renowned for his vituperative vinous veracity. Britain's *Guardian* newspaper referred to his style as "calculatedly distasteful." Waugh wrote about wine for magazines including *Tatler,* *Harpers and Queen* and the *Spectator.* He collected his wine writing in a 1987 book entitled *Waugh on Wine.* Like Amis, Waugh eschewed fruity and floral references. He was at his best in the art of evisceration, as evidenced by his description of a sought-after Spanish red wine: "This is the kind of heavy oak-vanilla taste that the Spanish think high-class but I prefer my Horlick's (British Ovaltine) without dust and cobwebs."

A red from the Languedoc region of Southern France was, for Waugh, "hairy and longbottomed." In response to the suggestion of notes of cherry fruit and smokiness in a Burgundy, Waugh noted, "I have been eating cherries all my life and breathing in smoke for much of it, but I have never found a Burgundy that tasted of either." Waugh once offered a wine description that was so offensive he was brought before the British Press Complaints Commission!

Waugh's cynical wit is most apparent in his hilarious suggestion that "wine writing should be camped up. . . bizarre and improbable side-tastes should be proclaimed: mushrooms, rotting wood, black treacle, burned pencils, condensed milk, sewage, the smell of French railway stations or ladies' underwear... anything to get away from the accepted list of fruit and flowers."

❦ Spiritual ❦

"Beauty captivates the flesh in order to obtain permission to go right through to the soul."
— Simone Weil (1909-1943), French Philosopher

In the *Gitanjali*, the Nobel Prize-winning poet Rabindranath Tagore (1861-1941) celebrates the senses as a means to transcendence. He explains that renunciation isn't his path to deliverance. Rather, he emphasizes:

"I feel the embrace of freedom in a thousand bonds of delight. Thou ever pourest for me the fresh draught of thy wine of various colors and fragrance, filling this earthen vessel to the brim."

Tagore continues:

"No, I will never shut the door of my senses. Yes, all my illusions will burn into illumination of joy, and all my desires ripen into the fruits of love."

Like Tagore, many mystics and spiritually oriented poets use the metaphor of wine to evoke the sacred. As poet Ivan Granger explains, "Sacred poetry traditions from all over the world compare ecstatic union with drunkenness." Founder of the Mevlevi order of Sufism, Jallaludin Rumi is renowned as one of the masters of sacred poetry. Rumi's poetry is awash with vinous imagery, a few examples among the many he penned are:

The lovers will drink wine night and day.
They will drink until they can
tear away the veils of intellect and
melt away the layers of shame and modesty.

And;

The grapes of my body can only become wine
After the winemaker tramples me.
I surrender my spirit like grapes to his trampling
So my inmost heart can blaze and dance with joy.

It's not unusual for participants in this exercise to experience a spiritual epiphany. Here's an example from a recent new symposium:

Remembering
I forget, every day I forget...
Sometimes for a week, sometimes for months, I forget...
But then a day like today happens...
The sun, bright warm, light, everywhere, the sun...
Then I remember, the smells, the tastes, the sights...
People laughing, talking, happy, the wine...
I remember, like the rays of the sun
We are connected, different but one.
Tomorrow, I will try to remember again.

❦ The Results ❦

"A man will be eloquent if you give him good wine."
—Ralph Waldo Emerson

This simple exercise leads groups to discover the truth of Greek poet Alcaeus' (c. 625 - c. 575 B.C.) observation: "Wine is a peep-hole on a man." Exploring wine with poetic language gently dismantles the wall of formality and stiffness to reveal a shared sense of our deeper humanity and potential for the creative.

Of course, some poems are better than others. These are the ones that, as David Whyte comments, "are able to speak to something universal yet personal and distinct at the same time; to create a door through which others can walk into what previously seemed unobtainable realms, in the passage of a few short lines."

Every now and then someone writes a poem in this exercise that meets these criteria, and the audience recognizes it immediately. But even, as in most cases, when this standard isn't achieved, it is the embrace of poetic awareness, and the sense of play and creative fun, that uplifts and unites the group.

David Whyte explains, "In a sense all poems are good; all poems are an emblem of courage and the attempt to say the unsayable."

Accessing poetry and the poetic spirit through this lighthearted, wine-inspired process consistently brings out the muse, and the amusing, in all kinds of groups. As poems are read aloud the participants all seem to deepen their appreciation for the capacity of each member for greater expressiveness and creativity. This shared glimpse of creative potential is inspiring and often surprising. After a recent wine and poetry event, the vice president in charge of a group of construction managers commented, "I was impressed by everyone's creativity, but I was especially amazed that the two most moving poems came from my information technology and finance people. I had no idea that they were that creative!"

The event encourages a level of soulful sharing that makes it easier for people to connect and deepen their personal bonds. The sense of personal connection and friendship is wonderful in purely social situations, and it also helps to nurture the informal innovation network in all kinds of organizations. Much of the real innovative thinking in an organization isn't sourced in formal meeting but rather through informal collaboration by people who like to work together and who share an inspiration for creative change. As many recent studies show, a group of ten people with high emotional intelligence (EQ) will consistently work more effectively and innovatively than a group of ten people chosen on the basis of high IQ. The combination of wine and poetry seems to enhance the EQ of those with high IQ.

Caveat! If you are conducting a session with a view to bringing different groups together, be sure to award prizes to representatives of each group. In a program for 125 senior managers from two very different companies who had just consummated a difficult merger, winners were initially chosen on the basis of merit alone. But since the purpose of the exercise was primarily to bring the team together, I took the executive vice-president in charge of the group aside and asked her if the ten winners represented a balanced distribution between the two groups. It turns out that all 10 were from one of the groups. So together we found the five best examples from the other company, and everyone lived happily ever after.

The liberating context of non-judgmental, right-hemisphere appreciation and the gentle transformation wrought by the wine itself yields a reliable experience of emotional openness and joy. Emotional openness isn't usually mentioned in organizational mission and value statements, but the quality of feeling is surprisingly important to the facilitation of the highest levels of performance in a wide range of disciplines.

In the old paradigm of work, feelings didn't matter, all that counted was thought and action. But it turns out that feelings drive our behavior and determine our level of performance. In their groundbreaking book, *Powered by Feel,* Doug Newburg and Jim Clawson demonstrate that the highest levels of human performance are driven by emotional congruity. In other words, high performers feel good about what they do. Newburg and Clawson describe how world-class performers, touring musicians, Olympic athletes, heart surgeons, high-growth executives, and aircraft carrier landing crews have learned how to manage how they feel in order to improve their performance. They note that positive feelings are also intrinsically rewarding. You don't have to be a world-record holder or a heart surgeon to recognize the importance of feeling good about what you do. The same principle holds true for teams. Feeling good about your colleagues translates into the kind of open communication and *esprit de corps* that facilitates creativity and innovation.

Dr. Raj Sisodia, author of *Firms of Endearment,* adds, "Today's most successful companies bring love, joy, authenticity, empathy, and soulfulness into their businesses and deliver emotional, experiential, and social value—not just profits." His research demonstrates how social coherence and humanistic values lead not only to greater personal fulfillment but also to higher and more sustainable profits. Sisodia says,

"The wine and poetry exercise is a perfect prescription for helping to bring a group together while promoting a more creative, positive culture."

The great creative thinkers have always appreciated the importance of these qualities. The ancient Greeks, the masters of the Renaissance, and the Founding Fathers all understood that wine drinking can serve as a delightful catalyst for inspired thinking.

All-Time Wine/Poetry Prize Winners

**"Let us celebrate the occasion
with wine and sweet words."**
—Plautus (c. 254-184 B.C.) Roman playwright

You can add to the inspiration of your New Symposium by asking different members of your group to read great poetry aloud.

The English Romantic poet John Keats (1795 – 1821) noted, "Poetry should please by a fine excess. It should strike the reader as a wording of his own highest thoughts and appear almost as a remembrance." He penned many exquisite, Bacchus-inspired poems that meet his own high standards. Among the most beautiful is this excerpt from *Hyperion:*

> *Knowledge enormous makes a God of me.*
> *Names, deeds, gray legends, dire events, rebellions,*
> *Majesties, sovran voices, agonies,*
> *Creations and destroyings, all at once*
> *Pour into the wide hollows of my brain,*
> *And deify me, as if some blithe wine*
> *Or bright elixir peerless I had drunk,*
> *And so become immortal.*

And this excerpt from Master of Wine Jancis Robinson's favorite wine-related poem, *Ode to a Nightingale:*

O, for a draught of vintage! that hath been
Cool'd a long age in the deep-delved earth,
Tasting of Flora and the country green,
Dance, and Provençal song, and sunburnt mirth!

O for a beaker full of the warm South,
Full of the true, the blushful Hippocrene,
With beaded bubbles winking at the brim,
And purple-stained mouth;
That I might drink, and leave the world unseen,
And with thee fade away into the forest dim.

In addition to being one of the great Romantic poets, Lord Byron (1788-1824) was a wine lover and innovator in vinous language, turning the words *claret* and *Champagne* into verbs in a letter he penned to a friend: "We clareted and champagned until 2…"

Four-time winner of the James Beard Award for wine writing, Natalie MacLean chooses these exquisite lines from Byron, written in 1808, as her favorite wine-related poetry:

I lived, I loved, I quaffed like thee
I died; let earth my bones resign
Fill up - thou canst not injure me;
The worm has fouler lips than thine.
Where once my wit, perchance, hath shone,
In aid of others let me shine;
And when, alas! our brains are gone,
What nobler substitute than wine ?

The great Chinese poet Li Po (701-762), known affectionately as "The Drunken Poet" for his many references to wine, was a wandering Taoist, who is said to have drowned when he tumbled out of his boat on the Yangtze River in a wine-dazed attempt to embrace the reflected light of the moon. Here a taste of his writing:

To drown the ancient sorrows,
We drank a hundred jugs of wine
There in the beautiful night.
We couldn't go to bed with the moon so bright.

Then finally the wine overcame us
And we lay down on the empty mountain—
The earth for a pillow,
And a blanket made of heaven.

Another Chinese master, Tao Chi'en (365-427) wrote these sweet words:

Old friends know what I like,
They bring wine whenever they come around.
We spread out and sit under the pines,
After several rounds we are drunk again.

Old men chatting away – all at once,
Passing the jug around–out of turn.
Unaware that there is a "self."
How do we learn to value "things."
We are lost in these deep thoughts,
In wine, there is a heady taste.

The magnificent Persian poet Hafiz (1320-1388) was a contemporary of Chaucer and Dante. Ralph Waldo Emerson referred to him as "a poet for poets." Like Rumi, Hafiz equates wine with spiritual energy and drunkenness with divine rapture.

Cupbearer, it is morning, fill my cup with wine.
Make haste, the heavenly sphere knows no delay.
Before this transient world is ruined and destroyed,
Ruin me with a beaker of rose-tinted wine.
The sun of the wine dawns in the east of the goblet.
Pursue life's pleasure, abandon dreams,
And the day when the wheel makes pitchers of my clay,
Take care to fill my skull with wine!
We are not men for piety, penance and preaching
But rather give us a sermon in praise of a cup of clear wine.
Wine-worship is a noble task, O Hafiz;
Rise and advance firmly to your noble task.

Another Persian master, Omar Khayyam, reminds us that sharing wine and poetry, and some bread and song, is heaven on earth:

Here with a Loaf of Bread beneath the Bough,
A Flask of Wine, a Book of Verse—and Thou
Beside me singing in the Wilderness—
And Wilderness is Paradise now.

Other all-time great wine poets include Rumi, the French "Prince of Poets" Pierre de Ronsard (1524-1585), Hilda Dolittle (H.D.)(1886-1961), and the Nobel Prize winner Pablo Neruda (1904-1973). See especially his deliciously erotic "Ode to Wine".

Characteristics of a Fine Wine and a Fine Mind:

Cultivated, balanced, complex, intense, focused, subtle, deep, original, and it improves with age.

[PART 4]

THE FINISH

"*The effect of the wine, however,*
was a gentle exhilaration,
which did not so speedily pass away."
—Nathaniel Hawthorne (1804-1864),
American novelist in *The Marble Faun*

The Best Resources
for Learning More
About Wine

The number of wine journals, critics, websites, seminars, consultants, and magazines seems to be proliferating exponentially. It's not possible to review all of them. The resources presented here are those that I have found most useful, informative, and amusing. They represent a diversity of opinion as to preferences for various styles of wine and different ways of writing about it. Some folks will only read the *Wall Street Journal*, *The National Review*, watch Fox News, and listen to Rush Limbaugh; others will limit themselves to the *New York Times*, *Mother Jones*, watching MSNBC, and listening to NPR; but if you want to be well-informed you read, watch, and listen to diverse resources. So it is with wine. Critics with high integrity and passion for wine can disagree wildly about a given wine or the quality of a vintage. If you can, read them all, drink, and decide for yourself.

Robert Parker Jr.

My uncle, Dr. Ben Kendall, has a wonderful wine cellar. As you enter, the first thing you see is his shrine. Just as yoga devotees put an image of their guru in a place of worship, Uncle Ben displays a framed photograph of Robert Parker. Ben discovered years ago something that thousands of wine lovers around the world have come to appreciate: A Parker recommendation is an oenological benediction.

Recently, it's become fashionable to criticize Parker. Some say that he has a bias toward wines that are big and intense and that he underrates the understated and the subtle. Some decry the numerical scale that he popularized, rating wines from 50-100 points, just like a grade in school. And others feel that he has too much influence on winemakers— that wines are becoming "Parkerized." In other words, wines are being made to please his palate so they can get a high score and therefore command a higher price.

But that's mostly just "sour grapes" from the envious. Of course, he isn't infallible and his approach isn't for everyone. His writing style, like his taste, is bold and assertive. Whether one agrees or disagrees with his ratings and descriptions, it's clear that Parker has set the benchmark for wine criticism. He may not be a guru, but he is a mensch. He works tirelessly, tasting thousands of wines every year, to help you find the very best. Ben Franklin said, "Wine is proof that God loves us and wants us to be happy." So does Parker. www.erobertparker.com

Karen Page and Andrew Dornenburg

Karen Page is a Harvard MBA and the former chairperson of the Harvard Business School Women's Alumni Association. Andrew Dornenburg is a world-class chef who cooked with Anne Rosenzweig at Arcadia. Together, they are the James Beard Award-winning authors of *Becoming a Chef, The Flavor Bible* and eight other outstanding books on food and wine. Their 2006 release, *What to Drink with What You Eat,* has become the definitive guide to food and wine pairing. *Publisher's Weekly* aptly refers to them as an "incisive, hip writing team." They also write the weekly wine column for the *Washington Post* and one of the most informative and engaging food/wine blogs on the planet. They bring a unique and powerful combination of business savvy, culinary sophistication, and oenological insight to their audiences. Watch for them to become Julia Child and James Beard 2.0! www.becomingachef.com

Kevin Zraly

Zraly is a pioneer in the field of wine education. He was one of the first educators to combine a serious knowledge of wine with a light-hearted and playful approach. He is the recipient of the James Beard Award and the author of the best-selling *Windows on the World Complete Wine Course*. If you want to get just one book to develop a practical appreciation of wine, this is it. Robert Parker says, "Kevin is the finest wine educator I have known, a naturally gifted speaker, exceptionally articulate, refreshingly humble, and candid." Zraly offers a number of programs that are particularly valuable for business groups, including his "One-Hour Wine Expert Course" and "Corporate Wine Dinner." www.windowswineschool.com

Wendy Dubit

Wendy Dubit served as a founding editor of *Wine Enthusiast* magazine and as the editor-in-chief of *Friends of Wine / Les Amis du Vin*. She also co-authored the chapter on *Wine Smelling 101* in Kevin Zraly's classic *Windows on the World Complete Wine Course*. As the originator of *The Senses Bureau*, Wendy offers a series of enjoyable experiences and exercises in savoring wine that she calls *The Wine Workout*. She explains, "Wine becomes a training ground for the senses, memory, and mind. *The Wine Workout* elucidates the multi-faceted magnificence that resides in each well-made bottle of wine — the embodiment of time and place, vines and grapes, soil and weather, nature and art — it also acknowledges that that's just where the beauty starts! Of equal wonder is what takes place within us when we experience wine — from anticipation to articulation, from awakened and enlivened senses to the creation, integration, and consolidation of memories." www.vergant.com, www.thesensesbureau.com

Natalie MacLean

A four-time winner of the James Beard Award for wine writing, Natalie MacLean was also named the "World's Best Drink Writer" at the World Food Media Awards. Her excellent website notes, "she credits the long line of hard drinkers from whom she descends for her ability to drink like a fish—and for the motivation to write about it, in a transparent attempt to make it look respectable." She offers an informative free newsletter, and her book *Red, White, and Drunk All Over: A Wine-Soaked Journey from Grape to Glass* is a pleasure to read. www.nataliemaclean.com

Ken Chase

Ken Chase likes to introduce himself to audiences by explaining, "I'm an oenologist. That's like a gynecologist with a wine twist." Known as the "Wine Guy of the Skies," Chase is the wine consultant for Air Canada and has consulted for Delta, Lufthansa, Cathy Pacific, and Malaysian Airlines. He also works as technical advisor to many great wineries. Chase apprenticed in the vineyards of France, Germany, and Italy and then studied at the University of California at Davis and holds a Master's degree in oenology and viticulture from the University of Melbourne. Fluent in French and German, Ken is an international ambassador for fine wine. His technical knowledge is unsurpassed and so is his sense of humor. Based in Canada, Chase is the Mike Myers of the wine world. Ken Chase c/o Kenology @cogeco.ca

Leslie Sbrocco

Sbrocco is a pioneer in Venus-oriented wine prose. Her first book, *Wine for Women: A Guide to Buying, Pairing and Sharing Wine*, won the Georges Duboeuf Wine Book of the Year award. Sbrocco hosts the innovative PBS wine and food television show *Check Please!* She is a charming, witty, and well-versed critic and guide to wine enjoyment and appreciation. Her most recent book is *The Simple & Savvy Wine Guide*. www.lesliesbrocco.com

Eddie Osterland

There are fewer than one hundred Master Sommeliers in the United States, and Osterland was the first. When he comes to the podium to address a large audience at a corporate dinner, he begins with a very convincing imitation of a French-accented wine snob. After a minute or so he shifts into his real persona: a friendly, funny knowledgeable guy from New Jersey who began to learn about wine while living in France thirty years ago. Eddie Osterland is the rare dinner speaker who can keep the audience's attention even after the drinking has commenced. He offers a number of excellent programs designed for business groups. www.eddieosterland.com

Wine Spectator

A monthly publication, *Wine Spectator* offers informative and entertaining interviews, features and articles. The *Spectator* employs a highly skilled staff of professional reviewers including: James Suckling, James Laube, Harvey Steiman, Bruce Sanderson, Thomas Matthews, Kim Marcus, and James Molesworth, each with a different regional specialty. Look for the initials of the reviewer next to the rating, and, as always, calibrate your taste with theirs. www.winespectator.com

Stephen Tanzer

Tanzer is the editor and publisher of the *International Wine Cellar*, a bimonthly independent wine journal. A former wine columnist for *Food and Wine* and *Forbes*, Tanzer tastes more than ten thousand wines each year.

Another devotee of the 100-point scale, Tanzer's palate and pen have been praised by Parker, Robinson, and the legendary head of Christie's wine department, Michael Broadbent, who comments, "What I like about the *Wine Cellar* is that the articles deal in reasonable depth with a couple of major subjects and appear to me to be extremely well balanced and sensible. Highly interesting and useful." www.wineaccess.com/expert/tanzer

Allen Meadows

"Burgundy is to wine," Jay McInerney observes, "what the Balkans are to geopolitics." That's why the world needs Allen Meadows. An executive in the world of finance for twenty-five years, Meadows retired in 1999 to pursue his passion: tracking down the best of Pinot Noir with hound-like devotion. He created www.burghound.com in 2001 to share the fruits of his quest with those who seek the best of the most fickle and elusive of all varietals. www.burghound.com

Mary Ewing-Mulligan

Mary Ewing-Mulligan, M.W., and her husband Ed McCarthy are

the authors of the classic bestseller *Wine for Dummies*. They've also penned, *Wine Style: Using Your Senses to Explore and Enjoy Wine*, a delightful book devoted to "Diversity in wine. Empowerment of wine drinkers." Mary Ewing-Mulligan was the first woman in America to become a Master of Wine. She has headed the International Wine Center, based in New York City, since 1984. The I.W.C. offers world-class wine education seminars and classes that enable students to earn internationally recognized credentials from the Wine & Spirit Education Trust ®. www.internationalwinecenter.com

Jancis Robinson

When Queen Elizabeth II wants to know which claret to have with her pheasant, she calls Jancis Robinson, the editor of *The Oxford Companion to Wine* and co-author with Hugh Johnson of *The World Atlas of Wine*. A wine-writer and presenter since 1975, Robinson earned the coveted Master of Wine title in 1984. She was also awarded an OBE (Officer of the British Empire) by the Queen in 2003. A captivating presenter, Robinson is forthright, perspicacious, and reliable. Her website offers a cornucopia of useful free advice for both the beginner and the aficionado. www.jancisrobinson.com

Hugh Johnson

Hugh Johnson is the author of the superb wine history book *Vintage: The Story of Wine* and co-author, with Jancis Robinson, of *The World Atlas of Wine*. He also offers an annual release: *Hugh Johnson's Pocket Wine Book*. Johnson's inspiration to write about wine came after a friend brought him two glasses and suggested a comparative tasting. Johnson notes, "One was magic and one was just ordinary. This caught my imagination." Johnson has written passionately in opposition to the 100-point scoring system and urges his readers to rely on their own independent judgment. In 2006, Johnson released an autobiographical book entitled, *A Life Uncorked*. In charming and poetic fashion he guides the reader to understand that wine is a special cultural phenomenon that is "about human relations, hospitality, bonding—all the maneuvers of social life—and all under the influence, however benign, of alcohol."

Michael Broadbent

Michael Broadbent is a legendary British wine writer and connoisseur. He became a Master of Wine in 1960 and the head of Christie's wine department in 1966. He offers sage advice on how to excel at identifying wine at blind tastings: "A sight of the label is worth fifty years experience." His book, *Michael Broadbent's Vintage Wine*, is a classic. Broadbent's son, Bartholomew, apprenticed with his dad and has become a world authority on Port and Madeira. Bartholomew founded Broadbent Selections, Inc., in 1996. www.broadbent.com

Clive Coates

Clive Coates is another renowned British Master of Wine. He published a superb independent fine-wine magazine, *The Vine*, from 1989 to 2005. Coates's recent books include *The Wines of Bordeaux* (2004), *The Great Wines of France* (2005), and *The Wines of Burgundy* (2008). www.clive-coates.com

Oz Clarke

When wine experts are asked "Of all your colleagues, who has the most refined palate?" many of them will mention Oz Clarke. A former Shakespearean actor, Clarke is as entertaining as he is knowledgeable. Renowned as something of a gustatory and olfactory prodigy, Clark excelled at blind-tasting competitions as a student at Oxford. He appears frequently on the BBC and co-hosts the popular TV series *Oz and James's Big Wine Adventure*. His books include *The Pocket Wine Book 2010* and *The Encyclopedia of Grapes*.

Gary Vaynerchuk

The founder of winelibrary.com, Vaynerchuk is also the author of *101 Wines Guaranteed to Inspire, Delight, and Bring Thunder to Your World* and *Crush It!*. A consummate salesman and innovator in the field of wine marketing and communication, Vaynerchuk presides over a rapidly growing $50 million business with more than one hundred employees. His passion, enthusiasm, authenticity, and in-depth knowledge of wine are expressed in his unique "Vaynercabulary." Although traditionalists revile him as the oenological anti-Christ, legions of "Vayniacs" are delighted by wine descriptors such as: "barbecue-esque," "OS" (Obnoxious Silkiness), "haunted house," "Tootsie Roll," "Pop Rocks," "Nesquik," "Grape Ape," "blueberry pancake topping at IHOP," and "Big League Chew." The method to his madness is his appeal to gustatory and olfactory images from childhood, a time when the senses were innocent and alive. Vaynerchuk eviscerates pretension and invites his fans and customers to make wine appreciation fun. www.winelibrarytv.com

Additional Recommended Resources

Anthony Dias Blue: ADB is a mega-maven of *la dolce vita*. www.bluelifestyle.com

Doug Frost: One of only a handful of experts to hold both the Master of Wine and Master Sommelier titles, Frost is the author of a number of fine books, including *On Wine: A Master Sommelier and Master of Wine Tells All*. www.dougfrost.com

The Wall Street Journal Guide to Wine by John Brecher and Dorothy J. Gaiter: Many folks buy the *Wall Street Journal* just to read their column.

The Wine Bible by Karen MacNeil: Hallelujah for this remarkably user-friendly vinous scripture.

The University Wine Course by Marian W. Baldy, Ph.D: A thorough, lucid wine appreciation, text and self-tutorial.

Laurie Forster, aka "The Wine Coach": Forster combines her savvy as a sommelier with her experience as a life coach to provide engaging, enjoyable wine events. Her book, *The Sipping Point*, is a short, sweet, and down-to-earth guide to the practical essentials of wine. www.thewinecoach.com

Wine and Philosophy: A Symposium on Thinking and Drinking by Fritz Allhoff: Plato would be pleased.

Educating Peter: How Anybody Can Become an (Almost) Instant Wine Expert by Lettie Teague: The wine editor for *Food & Wine* magazine initiates Peter Travers, the *Rolling Stone* film critic, into the world of the cognoscenti.

Great Wine Made Simple by Andrea (Immer) Robinson: One of only fourteen women in the world who have earned the title of Master Sommelier, also, a Master Smiler, Robinson is the "Ms. Congeniality" of the oenological universe. www.andreaimmer.com

Rosemary Zraly aka "The Champagne Lady": An effervescent ambassador for bubbly, Zraly is the author of *Champagne Uncorked! The Insider's Guide to Champagne!* www.champagnelady.com

A History of the World in 6 Glasses by Tom Standage: In addition to a brilliant chapter on wine this book offers a fascinating perspective on the role of beer, spirits, coffee, tea and coca-cola as cultural catalysts.

The Cork Jester's Guide to Wine by Jennifer Rosen: Fulfills its promise to help you "learn about wine while spitting it out your nose laughing." www.corkjester.com

Passion on the Vine: A Memoir of Food, Wine, and Family in the Heart of Italy by Sergio Esposito. Bill Buford, author of *Heat*, writes "the best book about Italian wine today, if only because Sergio Esposito understands that its mysterious greatness is in its poetry." www.italianwinemerchant.com

Bacchus & Me: Adventures in the Wine Cellar and *A Hedonist in the Cellar: Adventures in Wine* by Jay McInerney: A novelist (*Bright Lights, Big City*) and self-proclaimed chronic sufferer from a benign form of oenophilia, McInerney's passion for wine and his literary talent came together when he was asked to write the wine column for *House and Garden* magazine. These books are collections of his columns.

A Wine Miscellany by Graham Harding: A potpourri of wine curiosities.

Adventures on the Wine Route: A Wine Buyer's Tour of France by Kermit Lynch: An idiosyncratic trip through French wine with one of the great importers.

Reflections of a Wine Merchant by Neil Rosenthal: Another renowned importer, Rosenthal is a passionate terroirist who pulls no punches in sharing his story.

Oldman's Guide to Outsmarting Wine: 108 Ingenious Shortcuts to Navigate the World of Wine with Confidence and Style by Mark Oldman: Winner of the Georges Duboeuf "Best Wine Book of the Year Award" in 2005. www.markoldman.com

Decanter Magazine: A British-based wine magazine and website featuring regular columns from Michael Broadbent, Hugh Johnson, Stephen Spurrier, and many other wine luminaries. www.decanter.com

The Wine Enthusiast: Archived articles are available free on their site, which features a great catalogue for buying wine accoutrements. www.wineenthusiast.com

Wine & Spirits Magazine: A must-read for wine professionals and cognoscenti.

Robin Garr's Wine Lovers Page: The *New York Times* praises this Pulitzer Prize-winning journalist and wine lover for a free site that "outdoes all others for sheer quantity of friendly, well-written information about wine." www.wineloverspage.com

The Wine Doctor (hosted by Dr. Chris Kissack, a physician specializing in neo-natal medicine): Another free website featuring in-depth coverage of a wide range of topics. www.thewinedoctor.com

The Pour: The blog of Eric Aismov, pioneer of the *New York Times'* $25 and under dining column, and now chief wine critic for the *Times.* www.thepour.blogs.nytimes.com

Wine 2.0: The wine industry's innovator in social networking, focusing on the next generation wine consumer. www.winetwo.com

www.riedel.com: The best wine glasses in the world.
www.wine-searcher.com: Track down the wines you want.

Wine Geek Jargon Guide

Frank J. Prial wrote the "Wine Talk" column in the New York Times for twenty-five years until his retirement in 2005. Prial was devoted to demystifying wine and making its enjoyment more accessible. He coined the term "Winespeak" which he defined as "A peculiar subgenre of the English language … [it] has flowered wildly in recent years, like some pulpy jungle plant."

"Winespeak" is geek jargon. The Encarta World English Dictionary offers two definitions of the word *jargon*. The first refers to specialized language used by members of a group, "especially when the words and phrases are not understood or used by other people." The second definition is "pretentious or meaningless language."

Sometimes, wine jargon serves a useful purpose. Other times, it's used primarily to exclude and bully those who are unfamiliar with it.

This Wine Geek Jargon Guide doesn't aim to be a comprehensive guide to "Winespeak," rather it highlights some of the most useful, interesting, misused and amusing words as it empowers you to be impervious to wine snobs and bullies.

Aroma: The "primary" smell of the wine. The fragrance originating with the grapes.

Attack: The initial impression on the palate. It's hard not to want to give a wedgie or at least a noogie to people who use this term.

Backward: (synonym: "closed") A wine that is not yet ready to drink. The word suggests a young wine that will, with patience, become more accessible and enjoyable

Bead: Bubbles. A persistent flow of tiny bubbles is a sign of a high-quality sparkling wine. The average bottle of champagne contains almost 250 million bubbles, according to fizzicist Bruno Dutertre.

Biodynamic: An esoteric and effective method of viticulture pioneered by the founder of anthroposophy, Rudolf Steiner (1861- 1925). Biodynamic is to grape growing what a Waldorf School is to children. Now used by many of the world's great wineries including Larmandier-Bernier, Jacques Selosse, M. Chapoutier, Telmo Rodriguez, Pingus, Domaine Leroy, Joseph Phelps, Araujo Estates, and many others.

Blind-tasting: Tasting wine without knowing its identity. It doesn't require blindfolds, just brown paper bags and rubber bands to conceal the labels. Blind-tasting is fun when everyone wants to do it and agrees without being coerced. Although many wine writers rate their bottles blind, others are critical of the procedure. Kermit Lynch, the legendary importer of fine wine quips: "Blind tasting is to wine what strip poker is to love."

Body: George Bernard Shaw (1856-1950) was a wine-lover who despised milk. He quipped, " A mind of the caliber of mine cannot derive its nutrient from cows." Nevertheless, cows are helpful in understanding the term body. Cream is "full-bodied," regular milk is "medium bodied," and skim milk is "light-bodied." In other words, body is the impression of the fullness or weight of a wine in your mouth. Alcohol, dissolved solids, and glycerin combine to create these impressions.

Botrytis Cinerea: (a.k.a.Noble rot) This is a mold that vintners encourage on certain ripe white grapes. Botrytis shrivels the berry and the sweetness retreats, concentrating into fabulously flavorful droplets. These droplets are harvested in a painstaking process and then vinified to create great dessert wines like Sauternes.

Bouquet: The "secondary" smells of the wine. The more subtle and complex fragrances imparted by the aging process.

Breathing: (aka Aeration) Exposure to oxygen allows younger wines to open up and express their aromas and flavors. Older wines can often be more fragile and may fade quickly with exposure to air. Some wine professionals don't make a big deal about breathing or decanting, preferring to allow the wine to "open and evolve in the glass."

Brettanomyces: A hint of "barnyard," "sweaty saddle" or "wet dog" is sometimes considered desirable, but if your wine smells like dirty diapers, a pigsty, or used Band-Aids then its probably been infested by this wild yeast, nicknamed "Brett."

Brix: A measurement of the dissolved sucrose level in a wine. The name comes from A. F. W. Brix, a German chemist who devised a reliable scale for measuring the sugar content of grapes and wine.

Corked/Corky: If your wine smells like a musty basement or wet cardboard it's probably been tainted by trichloranisole (TCA). Up to 5 percent of wines with real cork stoppers may be affected. (It has nothing to do with crumbs of cork in your wine). When the server sez: "Howz yer wine, good? If it's corked just say, "T'aint."

Cooked: If you read *Kitchen Confidential* by Anthony Bourdain, you're familiar with some of the horrifying antics and unsanitary practices that take place behind the scenes of a restaurant. But, *cooked* doesn't refer to something the chef does with your wine, rather, it's more likely that the warehouse where the wine was stored was without air conditioning or that the delivery person left it in the truck for a few 95-degree days. If your wine has a blah, dull, overboiled stew quality then it has probably been improperly stored and "cooked."

Cult Wine: A small production wine that inspires aficionados to pay enormous prices.

Diurnal Temperature Difference (DTD): Grape quality and rate of ripening are influenced dramatically by the shift between day and night temperatures.

Dumb: Similar to "Backward," but with a more complex meaning: Sometimes a wine that is accessible and delicious in its first year or so in the bottle seems to "shut down." The fruit flavors aren't apparent, but the subtle nuances that come with age haven't yet emerged. Oenologists don't really understand this unpredictable, transitional, adolescent phase in the wine's evolution, but its best to wait for the wine to grow out of it.

> *"Superb wine, but it has its periods of recession. Like a foot which goes to sleep, has pins and needles, and then recovers."*
> Stephen Potter's tongue-in-cheek description of a "dumb" wine from his essay *"Winesmanship."*

Earthlings: Wine lovers who prefer earthy qualities in their glass.

> *"Think of earth as wine's birthmark, the thumbprint not of its maker but of its Maker."*
> —Jennifer Rosen, *The Cork Jester's Guide to Wine*

Forward: The opposite of backward. A wine that matures early and offers generous flavors, sometimes bordering on the flamboyant.

Fruit bomb: A wine with super-concentrated fruit aromas and flavors.

Fruitloopers: Wine lovers who prefer to drink "fruit bombs."

Grape nuts: Wine enthusiasts, also known as "Cork Dorks."

Jancisive: A pithy, insightful wine comment in the style of Jancis Robinson, M.W.

Examples of Jancisive comments include, *"Of all the classic French wine regions, the one that has changed most fundamentally over the last ten years is the one that looks the most set in medieval aspic, Burgundy."* And *"Among the well-established merchants, on the other hand, there are increasing signs of intelligent life..."*

Lees: The sediment- primarily dead yeast cells and small grape particles-that accumulates during fermentation and aging. Lees are usually removed by a process known as racking, but sometimes the wine is left in contact with the lees in an attempt to develop more flavor (the French call this *sur lie* which means "on the lees").

Maceration: The process of extracting color, aroma, and tannin by steeping the grape skins in wine after fermentation. Primarily used in making red wines.

"Where's the oenologist?" "He's macerating in the cellar."

Malolactic Fermentation: A process for converting malic acid (think Granny Smith apple) into lactic acid (think milk). Also known as "malo" or "ML" it makes wines softer, richer and sometimes more complex.

Master of Wine: A qualification and title, usually abbreviated to M.W., bestowed on those who have passed the rigorous examination sponsored by The Institute of Masters of Wine. There are fewer than three hundred M.W.s in the world.

Master Sommelier: A qualification and title, usually abbreviated to M.S., bestowed on those who have passed the rigorous examination sponsored by The Court of Master Sommeliers. There are fewer than two hundred Master Sommeliers in the world. The Master Sommelier program focuses on a broad beverage and service management curriculum, including aperitifs, cocktails, beer, after dinner drinks and cigars; while the Master of Wine emphasizes pure wine expertise. There are currently just three individuals who hold both titles.

Meniscus: The rim of the wine as it meets the glass. This term is only used by wine snobs and orthopedic surgeons.

Meritage: Clever marketing word for American Bordeaux-style blends. If it has "merit" and will improve with "age" it must be a "meritage." Although it's often mispronounced as the faux-French word it seems to be ("meritaj"), the correct sounding rhymes with "heritage." The first meritage was released by the precursor of the Cosentino Winery more than twenty years ago and was aptly named: "The Poet."

Must: The unfermented juice of freshly crushed grapes.

Oxidized: Oxidized is to wine as stale is to bread. The loss of freshness and flavor as the result of overexposure to air.

Riddling: Not a process of posing trick questions, *riddling* refers to a method developed by the Grand Dame of Champagne, Madame Cliquot, to ease the sediment out of champagne bottles.

Phylloxera: Vine-chomping louse.

Punt: Nothing to do with fourth down in football. It refers to the indentation at a bottle's bottom. Champagne bottles have deep punts to accommodate the extra pressure exerted by CO_2.

Sucrosuffication: The tendency to add unnecessary sweetness to food and wine in a way that suppresses natural flavors.

Sulfites: Sulfur dioxide is used by vintners everywhere to discourage bacterial formation and preserve wine. Sulfites are present in almost all wines and are only a problem for people with allergic sensitivities.

Screwage: Term coined by Jennifer Rosen, aka "The Cork Jester", referring to extremely high corkage fees.

Structure: (aka, "skeleton," "backbone" or "spine") A term for the scaffolding of a wine. A well-structured wine possesses an appropriate representation of acidity, alcohol, and tannin (in reds) to support its fruit.

Tannins: The mouth-puckering compounds imparted by the seeds, skins, and stems of grapes, as well as by oak barrels.

Tartrates: Tiny crystals of tartaric acid that sometimes appear in the bottom of your glass. They are harmless, odorless and taste-free. Many finer wines manifest these crystals because— in order to protect the more subtle, nuanced aspects of the wine's character— they haven't been overly-processed, cold-stabilized or filtered.

Ullage: The empty space in a bottle, barrel, or tank of wine.

Umami: First described by Chinese culinary masters more than twelve hundred years ago, umami was formally identified and named by Japanese scientist Dr. Kikunae Ikeda in 1908. Umami is the fifth taste, the others being sweet, salty, bitter, and sour. Truffles, morels, Iberico ham, parmesan cheese, sun-dried tomatoes, and soy sauce are all umami-rich. The tannins and oaky elements in some wines can have an umami character, and the effect of Botrytis can also be described this way. This term is guaranteed to impress your sommelier and wine-geek friends.

Viagrafication: The tendency to pump up the flavor volume and alcohol content of wines.

Zymology: The science of fermentation. Louis Pasteur was the first zymologist, but the word's origin can be traced to Nobel Prize-winning chemist Eduard Buchner (1860-1917) who discovered that fermentation was driven by the secretion of an enzyme that he christened *zymase*.

Top 10 Critical Wine-tasting Terms

The poet and wit Dorothy Parker (1893-1967) once said, " If you don't have anything nice to say then please come sit by me." When wine disappoints you can make the experience more enjoyable by finding just the right word to explain why. Here are a few favorites from the wine-tasters lexicon:

Attenuated: A wine bereft of body and fruit; on it's way to becoming *tired, dissipated, withered, decrepit* or *embalmed.*

Cabbagey: (aka, Skunky, Rubbery, Rancid) Unpleasant scents caused by an imbalance of volatile sulfuric compounds known as mercaptans.

Cloying: Webster's defines cloying as "distasteful by reason of excess, also excessively sweet or sentimental." When a wine doesn't have enough structure to support its fruit it can easily become cloying. A *flabby* wine is also short on structure but not quite overbearing enough to be called cloying.

Coarse: (aka, Awkward, Gross, Uncivilized, Barbaric, Ponderous, Rude) A rough quality in the texture of the wine, often associated with excessive tannins or oak.

Confected: A candylike aroma or flavor that seems manufactured and artificial. Not quite as bad as a wine that is *antiseptic, medicinal or pharmaceutical.*

Dirty: (aka, Vile, Filthy, Polluted, Excremental) Foul, unpleasant smells resulting from poor winemaking.

Hollow: (aka, Shallow, Vapid, Empty) A wine that promises some satisfaction as it enters the palate and doesn't seem to be bad on the finish yet is somehow lacking flavor in between.

Insipid: This word derives from the Latin *sapidus,* meaning "savory" and *sapere,* meaning "to taste." An insipid wine lacks savor and taste. It is watery, without heft, weight or sufficient structure. It can also be described as *anemic, anorexic, thin, flat, banal* or *wimpy.*

Over-oaked: When the smoky, woody, vanillin elements dominate the smell and taste of the wine.

Stemmy: (aka, Stalky or Green.) An overly astringent, harsh, grassy quality often caused by leaving the stems in the juice for too long or by underripe grapes.

Top 10 Positive Wine-Tasting Terms

As you delight in creating your own positive analogies, metaphors, and similes for the experience of wine it's also good to know some standard wine terms to express your enjoyment. Favorites include:

Balanced: The greatest wines integrate all their elements seamlessly and can leave the taster speechless with delight.

Chewy: (aka, Fleshy, Meaty) Wines that are mouth-filling, rich, dense, intense.

Complex: A wine that offers many nuances, subtleties and layers of flavor. A complex wine invites contemplation.

Deep: (aka, Concentrated, Highly-extracted) A fine wine possesses a depth of flavor, whether it is light, medium or full-bodied.

Elegant: A distinctive, harmonious wine that displays finesse, elan, and panache. It manages to be rich with flavor while possessing an ineffable lightness.

Luscious: A creamy, lush, buttery aroma and texture.

Perfumed: A fragrant, ethereal bouquet.

Robust: (aka, Big, Brawny, Muscular, Massive, Hefty, Imposing, Mesomorphic, Studly) Describes powerful red wines that are full-bodied with strong tannins and intense flavor.

Supple: A wine that is both easy to drink and complex.

Velvety: An opulent, smooth, lush texture. Brits say *silky* and the French call it *velouté.*

Top 10 Neutral Descriptors

In the hilarious essay *Winesmanship,* satirist Stephen Potter explains that the best way to bluff your way through a wine conversation is to say something boldly meaningless.

If you don't know what to say about a wine, you can always say that it is:
Affable
Amusing
Curious
Drinkable
Exemplary
Interesting
Intriguing
Representative
Typical
Vinous

Guide to British Wine Terms

In the early 1990s I was invited to lead a three-day retreat on Creative Thinking for the senior scientists of a global pharmaceutical company. When the human resource director was introducing the program to our group of Ph.D. biochemists and pharmacologists, he explained that he "didn't have to be a rocket scientist" to make the arrangements. One member of the group quipped in response, "Rocket science? What a lowly form of science. We use the term as a pejorative."

Then the leader of the group, a British gentleman, introduced me as follows, "This is Mr. Michael Gelb, he intends to teach *us* about thinking. Good luck, Mr. Gelb."

The seminar was filled with lively interaction and learning, and we enjoyed exceptional wines each evening. It was clear that it was a success when at the end the leader commented, in front of the whole group, "I must say, that was not bad, not bad at all."

While living in England for eight years, I developed a special fondness for British wit, understatement, and taste. Since George Bernard

Shaw referred to the United States and Britain as "Two cultures separated by a common language," here's a brief guide to British wine terms:

Austere: Wines that are understated, restrained, appropriate.

Brill: Brilliant.

Claret: Red wines from Bordeaux. Many years ago, when British lords were buying up most of the production, these wines were lighter in color than they are today. (The Brits actually controlled Bordeaux from the time Eleanor of Aquitaine hooked up with Henry Plantagenet (1152) until the end of the Hundred Years' War (1453).)

> *"How I like claret! It fills one's mouth with a gushing freshness, then goes down to cool and feverless; then, you do not feel it quarrelling with one's liver. No; 'tis rather a peace-maker, and lies as quiet as it did in the grape. Then it is as fragrant as the Queen Bee, and the more ethereal part mounts into the brain, not assaulting the cerebral apartments, like a bully looking for his trull, and hurrying from door to door, bouncing against the wainscott, but rather walks like Aladdin about his enchanted palace, so gently that you do not feel his step."* — John Keats

Champers: Champagne. "Let's pop down to Roddy's (Harrods) for some Champers."

Cheers: An all-purpose toast, also used to say "thanks" or "goodbye".

Corking: Excellent. A synonym for "spiffing." Usually used with a soupcon of sarcasm.

Frightfully immature: A wine that Americans or Australians consider properly aged and ready to drink.

Grip: A reference to the firm, positive structure of a wine.

Jolly: An adjective equivalent to *very*, as in, "This claret has jolly good grip."

Not bad: Awesome.

Oak-Bloke: A wine lover who prefers highly oaked wines (In the United States these folks are sometimes called "Woodchucks," "Beavers or "Termites").

Pips: Grape seeds, pits.

Plonk: Generic wine

Pudding wine: Dessert wine

Quite nice: Dreadful.

Ready: Used to refer to wines that are, by American or Australian standards of taste, so old that they posses only homeopathic remnants of flavor.

Racy: Pleasant, bracing acidity and bright flavors in a crisp white wine.

Wanker: aka Tosser—A self-referential wine snob, not a master of his Domaine.

French, Italian, Spanish and German Terms

Why is Merlot one of the most popular varietal wines in the United States? Is it because Merlot is relatively soft, supple and easy to like? Or is it because it's easy to pronounce?

The fear of embarrassment is the biggest inhibitor of adult learning. And mispronouncing a word or phrase can be so embarrassing to many folks that they don't bother to try. This guide to the foreign language terms used in this book will help you master the pronunciation of wine-related words in French, Italian, German, and Spanish.

Of course, sometimes its appropriate to pronounce a word from another language as a native speaker would and other times its best to say it in "Americanized" fashion. After reviewing the list below you will know the difference and have the choice of how to pronounce.

FRENCH

No matter how good you become at pronouncing these French terms the French will still pretend they don't understand you. But your *savoir faire* with anyone other than the French will be *magnifique*.

Appellation Controlee: (ahp-ehl-ah-see-ohn cone-troh-lay) A designation of a wine's regional authenticity. (The literal translation is "name control.") The French introduced this standard in the 1930s and it has become a model for the rest of the world.

Barrique: (bahr-eek) A fifty-nine-gallon oak barrel.

Blanc de Blancs: (Blahn-duh-blahn) Champagne from 100% Chardonnay grapes.

Brut: (broot) Dry champagne or sparkling wine. (Extra-Dry, Sec, Demi-Sec and Doux are all sweeter)

Cabernet Sauvignon: (cab-ehr-nay soh-veen-yohn) The primary grape of Bordeaux (usually blended with Merlot, Cabernet Franc, and Petite Verdot).

Chambertin: (shahm-behr-tahn] One of the legendary vineyards of Burgundy. Along with Champagne, this was Napoleon's favorite wine. He proclaimed, "Nothing makes the future look so rosy as to contemplate it through a glass of Chambertin." (Top producers include Claude Dugat, Domaine Leroy, Christophe Roumier)

Champagne: (shahm-pahn) The distinctive sparkling wine of France's Champagne region. In the classic film *Wayne's World* the beautiful Cassandra says, "I don't believe I've ever had French Champagne before."And Benjamin Kane, played by the wickedly unctuous Rob Lowe, responds, "Oh, actually all Champagne is French, it's named after the region. Otherwise it's sparkling white wine. Americans of course don't recognize the convention so it becomes that thing of calling all of their sparkling white Champagne, even though by definition they're not."

Although wonderful sparkling wines are emerging from California, Oregon, Italy, Spain, and other regions, Champagne reigns supreme in the world of vinous effervescence.

The legendary culinary innovator Georges Auguste Escoffier (1836-1935) asked the great actress Sarah Bernhardt (1844-1923) the secret of her inexhaustible energy. Bernhardt replied. *"The main thing is will power, sustained by an excellent champagne."*

Mark Twain quipped: *"Too much of anything is bad, but too much Champagne is just right."* And Oscar Wilde observed: *"Pleasure without champagne is purely artificial."* (Top producers include Krug, Bollinger, and Vilmart.)

Chardonnay: (shar-doh-nay) The basis of the exquisite whites of Burgundy such as Montrachet, Meursault and Chablis; it is also a key component of Champagne.

Chateuneuf du Pape: (Shah-toh-nuff doo pahp) Literally: "The new house of the Pope." A Southern Rhone wine of great complexity and power. (Top producers include Chateau Beaucastel, Vieux Telegraph, Henri Bonneau).

Condrieu: (Kohn-dree-uh) A region near the right bank of the Rhone River in France that is the source of great viognier.

> *"Ah, the white wine of Condrieu! Cool, supple on the tongue, it will surprise you with its indefinable taste, almost reminiscent of an apple. When you are finished drinking you'll discover that a little miracle has occurred-the sun, which generously bathes the vineyards, is now within you."*
> —Fernand Point

Cru: (Croo) "Growth." In Bordeaux, the highest quality wines are Premier Cru (first growth) in Burgundy the top designation is Grand Cru (great growth).

Dosage: [doh-sahj]A mixture of sugar, brandy or wine that's added to Champagne to induce a secondary fermentation in the bottle.

Garrigue: (Gah-reeg) The southern Rhône Valley and Provence equivalent of chaparral. Wines from this area are often redolent of lavender, thyme, sage, rosemary and earth.

Gout de Terroir: (Goo duh tear-wahr) "The taste of the soil." Refers to the special characteristics imparted by a particular vineyard and its microclimate. The French novelist and wine-lover Colette mused: "The vine makes the true savor of the earth intelligible to man. With what fidelity it makes the translation! It senses, then expresses, in its clusters of fruit the secrets of the soil."

> *"Different places on the face of the earth have different vital efflu-ence, different chemical exhalation, different polarity with differ-ent stars, call it what you like. But the spirit of the place is a great reality."*—D.H. Lawrence on terroir.

Je ne sais quoi: (Jzun say kwah) All-purpose wine description term. As Mike Myers might say, "This Chateau du Plonque has a certain I don't know what."

Les yeux de crapaud: (Lehzyuh duh krapoh) Literally "toad's eyes," this is a less than complimentary term for ungainly, large bubbles in a sparkling wine.

Méthode Champenoise: (met-tohd shahm-pen-wahz) The process developed to facilitate a second fermentation in the bottle, re-sulting in delightful flavor-concentrating tiny bubbles.

Mis en bouteille au château: (Meez ahn boo-taye oh shah-toh) Estate bottled.

Negociant: (nay-goh-syahn) A wine merchant who purchases the pro-duction of smaller growers and vintners and then sells it under his own label.

Sauvignon Blanc: (Soh-veen-yohn blahn) A key component of white Bordeaux and Sancerre, this varietal was revitalized in the United States by Robert Mondavi who dubbed it "Fume' Blanc." In the last 20 years New Zealand has emerged as one of the great sources for this bracing, food-friendly wine. (Top producers include Didier Dagueneau, Edmund Vatan, Lucien Crochet.)

Sauternes: (soh-tehrn) The exquisite "botrytisized" sweet white wine of Bordeaux, made primarily with the semillon grape, along with small amounts of Sauvignon Blanc. Chateau D'Yquem is the supreme example of Sauternes. (Other top producers include Climens, Raymond-Lafon and Rieussec.)

Sommelier: (Soh-meh-lyeh) A wine steward. A good sommelier should have the sensitivity of a family therapist, the poise of an aikido black belt, the stamina of a marathoner and an encyclopedic knowledge of wine.

Viognier: (Vee-oh-nyeh) The only grape used for the northern Rhône appellation of Condrieu. It is sometimes added to bring a touch of finesse to the syrah in Côte Rotie. (Top producers include Guigal, Yves Cuilleron and Chateau Grillet.)

ITALIAN

La dolce vita is delightfully expressed in *la bella lingua* (the beautiful language). Italians usually appreciate your efforts to speak their language.

Barbaresco: (bahr-ba-reh-sko) "The queen of wines." A graceful, feminine expression of the nebbiolo grape. (Top producers include Bruno Giacosa, Angelo Gaja, Produttorri di Barbaresco.)

Barolo: (bah-roh-loh) "The king of wines." A more masculine, powerful expression of the nebbiolo grape. (Top producers include Domenico Clerico, Roberto Voerzio, and Giussepe Mascarello.)

Brunello di Montalcino: (broo-neh-loh dee mohn-tahl-chee-noh) One of the great red wines of Italy made from a special clone of Sangiovese known as "Grosso." In the 1960s there were only 11 producers and now there are more than 200. (Top producers include Siro Pacenti, Fuglini, and Uccelliera.)

Chianti: (kee-ahn-tee) The classic Sangiovese based red wine of Tuscany. (Top producers include Antinori, Castello d'Ama, and Monsanto.)

Denominazione di Origine Controllata e Garantita: Commonly refered to as DOC (Dohk) A designation of a wine's regional authenticity. The Italian version of "Appellation Controlee."

Frizzante: (free-zhan-ta) Wines with light effervescence, slightly sparkling. *Pétillant* (pay-tee-yawn) in French and *spritzig* in German.

Nebbiolo: (neh-bee-oh-loh) *Nebbia* is the Italian for "fog." In the Langhe region of Italy the hot sunny summer days give way cool evenings and early morning fogs. The dramatic temperature shift (DTD) locks in the flavor of the grapes and prevents them from over-ripening. Despite noble attempts in other parts of the world the Nebbiolo based wines of Piemonte are in class by themselves.

Podere: [poh-day-reh] (also Fattoria, Tenuta) A farm or estate.

Sangiovese: (sahn-joe-veh-say) The name *Sangiovese* comes from the Latin *sanguis Jovis* meaning "the blood of Jove." Jove, aka Zeus, was the king of the gods, and Sangiovese is the reigning varietal in Tuscany. Brunello di Montalcino is 100 percent Sangiovese (a special clone) and Chianti is comprised of at least 90%. Sangiovese is also a key ingredient in many Super-Tuscans.

La bella lingua is a deliciously mellifluous language. Italian words are ideal for describing the experience of wine. Here are a few Italian wine-tasting terms to get you started. Experiment with expressive gestures as you practice pronouncing each word:

Carezzevole (kah-reh-seh-voh-lay)-Caresses your palate.

Generoso (jen-neh-roh-so)-Easy to appreciate, rich in flavor.

Rotondo (roh-tohn-doh)-Mellow and full, no rough edges.

Sapore del terreno di origine (sah-poor-reh dehl teh-rreh-noh dee oh-reej-eneh)-Earthy, redolent of the land (Italian for "Gout de Terroir").

Passato (pah-sa-toh)-Past it.

Peronosporato (pehr-oh-no-spore-ah-toh)-Mildewy.

Putrido (poo-tree-doh) -Bilge water.

Puzzolente (poo-tzoh-lehn-tay)-Foul.

SPANISH

Spain is a consistent source for great wines and great wine bargains.

Bodega: (boh-deh-gah) A winery.

Cava: (cah-vah) Sparkling wine.

Crianza: (cree-ahn-tza) A quality classification. Crianza reds are aged for two years, with a minimum of one year in wood (oak barrels).

Cosecha: [coh-seh-chah] Vintage.

Garnacha: (gar-nah-chah) This Spanish grape found its way to France when the papacy was centered in Avignon. Known as Grenache by the French, it is a prime component of Chateauneuf du Pape, and of the increasingly popular, and expensive, Spanish wines from Priorato.

Gran Reserva: (grahn ray-zer-vah) Gran Reserva reds are aged for five to seven years, with a minimum of two years in wood.

Jumilla: (who-mee-yah) This region was formally recognized in 1996. The Monastrell grape (Known as Mouvedre in France) thrives here and there are many great bargains available. The wines from Bodegas El Nido are mind-blowingly lush and powerful yet balanced.

Reserva: (ray-zer-vah) Reserva reds are aged for three years, with a minimum of one year in wood.

Ribera del Duero: (ree-behr-ah dehl doo-ehr-oh) Since it's official designation in 1982 the Ribera del Duero has risen to become one of the great regions of Spain and the world. (Top producers include Abadia Retuerta, Tinto Pesquera, and the legendary Vega-Sicilia.)

Rioja: (ree-oh-ha) The classic wine region of Spain. (Leading bodegas include Artadi, Fernando Remirez de Ganuza, and Muga.)

Tempranillo: (tehm-prah-nee-yoh)-An indigenous Spanish grape, it is the heart of the red wines from Rioja and Ribera del Duero.

Tertulia (ter-tulja) The Spanish equivalent of a symposium.

GERMAN

When ordering German wines its best just to point. By the time you finish saying some of these terms the wine will be well-aged. As Kingsley Amis quips: " A German wine label is one of the things life is too short for." German wine language reflects the national predilection for putting things in clearly organized categories.

Abfüllung: (ahb fool-ungh) "Bottled by."

Amtliche Prüfnummer: (ahmt-leekeh proof-noom-ehr) A code number granted to each bottle of quality wine.

Auslese: (ow-ss-layz-uh) "Select harvest" wines made of ripe, late-harvested grapes.

Beerenauslese: (beer-ehn-owss-layz-uh) "Harvest of selected berries." Individually picked "botrytised" grapes generate a wine with an exotic, rich, and honeyed quality.

Einzellag: (eye-n-zehl-agh) Single vineyard sites. Wines from these sites represent the pinnacle of German quality wine.

Eiswein: (ice-vine) A sweet wine made from frozen grapes.

Gutsabfüllung: (goot-zab-fool-ungh) Estate-bottled

Kabinett: (cah-bee-net) Light, off-dry wines. The vintage's first harvest.

Qualitat mit Pradikat: (kwa-lee-taht mitt preh-dee-kaht) "Quality with distinction," includes Germany's best wines.

Riesling: (reez-ling) The favorite white wine grape of many connoisseurs. Riesling is renowned for its aging potential and the way it expresses its terroir. Indigenous to Germany, it is now produced around the world in many styles, from crisp and dry to unctuous and sweet. (Top producers include Dr. Loosen, J.J. Prum and Peter Nicolay).

Sekt: (Sehkt) Sparkling wine

Spätlese: (shpeht-layz-uh) "late harvest." Spatlese grapes are picked after the Kabinett and before the Auslese harvest.

Trocken: (troh-kehn) "dry."

Trockenbeerenauslese: (troh-kehn beer-ehn-nowz-layz-uh) TBA "harvest of selected dry berries." Made from grapes affected by noble rot. TBA wines are produced in very small quantities, and are among the greatest sweet wines of the world. (Top producers include Muller-Catoir, Robert Weil and Selbach-Oster.)

Closing Poem:
Get Drunk

by Charles Baudelaire (1821-1867), French Romantic poet.

If we take Baudelaire's advice metaphorically then *Get Drunk* is an invitation to open our "right minds," allowing deeper passion, creativity, intuition and soulfulness.

Always be drunk.
That's it!
The great imperative!
In order not to feel
Time's grave burden
bruise your shoulders,
grinding you into the earth,
Get drunk and stay that way.
On what?
On wine, poetry, virtue, as you desire.
But get drunk.
And if you sometimes happen to wake up
on the porches of a palace,
in the green grass of a ditch,
in the dismal loneliness of your own room,
your drunkenness gone or disappearing,
ask the wind,
the wave,
the star,
the bird,
the clock,
ask everything that flees,
everything that groans

or rolls
or sings,
everything that speaks,
ask what time it is;
and the wind,
the wave,
the star,
the bird,
the clock
will answer you:
"Time to get drunk!
Don't be martyred slaves of Time,
Get drunk!
Stay drunk!
On wine, virtue, poetry, as you desire!"

Acknowledgments

Please get a glass of wine and join me in toasting to everyone who contributed to the creation of this book:

"C'ent Anni" to the wine experts who graciously shared their expertise: Ken Chase, Kevin Zraly, Craig Williams, Jancis Robinson, Gary Vaynerchuk, Leonardo LoCascio, Karen Page, Andrew Dornenburg, Natalie MacLean, Eddie Osterland, Leslie Sbrocco, Laurie Forster, Jan Shrem, Rosemary Zraly, Wendy Taylor, Chris Coad, Aimée Lasseigne, Jim Cook, Terry Thiese, Wendy Dubit, and Robert Parker Jr..

"Salud" to the physicians who reviewed the chapter on Wine and Health: Dr. Todd LePine, Dr. Donald Hensrud, Dr. Leonard Shlain, Dr. Marvin Hyett, Dr. Dale Schusterman, Dr. Jill Baron, Dr. Tereza Hubkova, and Dr. Bob Friedman.

"Skal" to all who contributed poetically: Emily Hickey, Lane Steinberg, Ivan Granger, Richard Eckel, Sally Rosenberg, Matt Burk, Bobby Kishore, David Whyte, Ted Hughes, Mitch Priestly, Aaron Crowley, Jim Karkanias, and Sonia Carlson.

"Cheers" to my colleagues and friends in the world of creativity and creative organizational development: Professor James Clawson, Sam Horn, Dan Pink, Ron Gross, Professor Raj Sisodia, Sir Ken Robinson, Wendy Palmer, SARK, Vanda North and Jill Badonsky.

"Prosit" to the scholars, musicians and artists who contributed to the chapters on Genius, Art and Music: Dava Sobel, Ross King, Professor William Wallace, Professor Bill Cook, Professor Martin Kemp, GrandMaster Raymond Keene, Professor Elaine Ruffolo, Stacy and Jerry Siena, Tony Barrese, Abbie Conant, Don Campbell, Ron Helman, Bill Horwedel, and Valentino Monticello.

"L'chaim" to my dear friends and family who read and critiqued the manuscript at various stages of evolution: Dr. Sanford Gelb, Joan

Gelb, Virginia Kendall, Dr. Marvin Hyett, George Cappannelli, David Kendall, Barbara Horowitz, and Peggy Dugas.

"Nastrovya" to my perspicacious editor Jennifer Kasius and the entire team at Running Press including Bill Jones, Craig Herman, Nicole DeJackmo, and Chris Navratil.

"A hej, hej hej" to Tony Buzan for his poetry and for sharing many great wines over the years.

"Zivio Ziveli" to a true artist, my gifted, illustrious friend, Carol Rose Brown

"Zum Wohl" to Tom Means, Ph.D, of The Means Language Center, who generously provided the phonetic pronunciation of the foreign language words in the book. (www.meanslanguagecenter.com)

"Saludos" to Wendy Dubit and to Karen Page and Andrew Dornenburg for their very special contributions to this project.

"Here's looking at you" to my sweetheart, Deborah Domanski. We met on an Alexander Technique retreat in Santa Barbara. I walked into what I thought was an empty room and she was sitting in the corner next to the fireplace. When I asked her what she was doing she replied that she was copying out some of her favorite poems into her journal. We soon discovered that we both particularly loved the poems of Rumi, Neruda, Tagore and Rilke. The next day she gave me a card with an inscription from a poem by Rilke.

> *"But if you'd try this: to be hand in my hand*
> *as in the wineglass the wine is wine.*
> *If you'd try this."*

One month later we had our first date when she came to New York for her Carnegie Hall debut. I made her dinner and served a 1997 Ciacci Piccolimini Brunello di Montalcino. In a natural and poetic fashion she described the wine in a way that deepened my appreciation of it, and of her. We've been together ever since.

Wine Drinking for Inspired Thinking Creative Notebook

*"Feathers shall raise men even as they do
birds, toward heaven; that is by letters written
with their quills."*
—Leonardo da Vinci,
on the value of keeping a notebook

What do Leonardo DaVinci, Thomas Edison, Marie Curie, and Albert Einstein all have in common? They all kept notebooks or journals. One of the distinguishing differences between average people and geniuses is that when an average person wakes up at 4 am with a quirky idea, they think, "I'm no genius," and they roll over and go back to sleep. But when Leonardo DaVinci arose at 4 am with an offbeat idea he wrote it down in his notebook. (In 1994, Bill Gates paid $30.8 million dollars for 18 pages of Leonardo's notebooks!)

If you must write for your job, then chances are that your work must be linear and left-brained, and your writing will be reviewed and judged by others. The beauty of a Creative Notebook is that it can be non-linear and more right-brained. Best of all, it's personal and confidential. You can use it to get your creative juices flowing, and to enhance the memory and pleasure of the wines you enjoy.

Please use these last few pages to begin your own "Wine Drinking for Inspired Thinking Creative Notebook." Use this space to record the names of wines you enjoy (you can paste in wine labels if you like) and then make comments, note your impressions, and play with your own poetic musings and/or creative doodling.

Cheers!

Name of Wine

Comments, Inspirations, and Poetic Musings

Name of Wine

Comments, Inspirations, and Poetic Musings

Name of Wine

Comments, Inspirations, and Poetic Musings

Name of Wine

Comments, Inspirations, and Poetic Musings

Name of Wine

Comments, Inspirations, and Poetic Musings

Name of Wine

Comments, Inspirations, and Poetic Musings

Name of Wine

Comments, Inspirations, and Poetic Musings

Name of Wine

Comments, Inspirations, and Poetic Musings

Name of Wine

Comments, Inspirations, and Poetic Musings

Name of Wine

Comments, Inspirations, and Poetic Musings